D1560927

Don Troiani's

GETTYSBURG

Don Troiani's
GETTYSBURG

36 Masterful Paintings and Riveting History
of the Civil War's Epic Battle

Don Troiani
Tom Huntington

STACKPOLE
BOOKS
celebrating 90 *years*

Published by Stackpole Books

An imprint of The Rowman & Littlefield Publishing Group, Inc.

4501 Forbes Blvd., Ste. 200

Lanham, MD 20706

www.rowman.com

Distributed by NATIONAL BOOK NETWORK

800-462-6420

British Library Cataloguing in Publication Information available

Library of Congress Cataloging-in-Publication Data

Name: Huntington, Tom, 1960–, author. | Huntington, Tom.
Title: Don Troiani's Gettysburg : 36 masterful paintings and riveting history of the Civil War's epic
    battle / Don Troiani, Tom Huntington.
Description: Guilford, Connecticut : Stackpole Books, [2019] | Includes bibliographical references.
Identifiers: LCCN 2018052447 (print) | LCCN 2018053705 (ebook) | ISBN 9780811768368 (electronic) |
    ISBN 9780811738354 (cloth : alk. paper) | ISBN 9780811738361 (pbk. : alk. paper)
Subjects: LCSH: Gettysburg, Battle of, Gettysburg, Pa., 1863—Pictorial works. | United States—History—
    Civil War, 1861–1865—Pictorial works. | United States—History—Civil War, 1861–1865—Art and
    the war.
Classification: LCC E475.53 (ebook) | LCC E475.53 .H893 2019 (print) | DDC 973.7/349—dc23
LC record available at https://lccn.loc.gov/2018052447

Printed in the United States of America

Contents

Foreword . . . . *vii*

Introduction 1
Brandy Station Review 27
The Battle of Brandy Station 30
The Gray Comanches 33
McPherson Ridge 36
"For God's Sake Forward" 39
The Unconquered 42
The Fight for the Colors 44
The Boy Colonel 47
Generals Robert E. Lee and A. P. Hill 51
Iron Brigade, 24th Michigan Volunteers 53
The Black Hats 56
General J. B. Gordon at Gettysburg 59
Cemetery Hill 62
Battle in the Streets 65
Decision at Dawn 67
"The Men Must See Us Today" 70
Berdan's Sharpshooters 73
Confederate Sharpshooter 76
Saving the Flag 79
Don't Give an Inch 83
Little Round Top 86
Lions of the Round Top 89
Barksdale's Charge 92
Retreat by Recoil 95
The First Minnesota 98
1st Minnesota Volunteer Infantry 101
Band of Brothers 104
Newhall's Charge 107
"Come On, You Wolverines!" 109
Hampton's Duel 112
The Civilians of Gettysburg 115
The Emmitsburg Road 118
Toward the Angle 121
Rock of Erin 124
The High-Water Mark 127
"Give Them Cold Steel, Boys" 130

Foreword

O N THE MORNING OF JULY 2, 1863, THE SECOND DAY OF THE BATTLE OF
Gettysburg, Robert E. Lee gathered his top lieutenants to hear their
thoughts on the attack he was planning. It was a sight to behold. As the
dawn fog lifted, James Longstreet, Lee's trusted senior corps commander, sat on
a log whittling. Rookie corps commander A. P. Hill attended, as did Henry Heth,
his head bandaged, and John Bell Hood, hours away from a devastating wound.
A foreign observer sporting a top hat climbed a tree while another stood nearby
in full hussar regalia. A "care-worn" Lee, dressed in his prim finest, presided.

The moment was memorable for reasons more consequential than the
imagery. Since reaching Gettysburg the evening before, Longstreet had opposed
taking the offensive, preferring to maneuver and force George Meade to attack,
a preference he repeated this morning. But Lee's mind was made up: the attack
was to proceed under Longstreet, who dragged, or seemed to drag, his boots
before launching the assault. Ever after, Longstreet would be dogged by accusa-
tions of insubordination and delay and would sometimes be blamed for Confederate defeat at Gettysburg and—if this battle was indeed the turning point—in
the Civil War itself.

It is no surprise that this visually and historically compelling scene seized the
imagination of Don Troiani, who depicted it in *Decision at Dawn*, one of the dozens of his Gettysburg paintings collected in this book.

The battle of Gettysburg is a patchwork of moments like this: scenes of drama
and decision, courage and consequence; scenes of unforgettable imagery of both
landscapes and human endeavor; scenes that fire the imagination, that remind
us what ordinary men can do for cause and comrade, that awe as well as appall.
As one veteran reflected two decades after his regiment was mauled on July 1,
"Dread scenes must rise before our eyes as heroic action illumines every place;
therefore, Gettysburg is resplendent."

Tom Huntington describes many of these moments in the narrative that
follows and reminds us of the uncertainty and misconception that still surround
so many aspects of Gettysburg, from who fired the first shots, to whether the 20th
Maine's famous bayonet charge was as tide-turning as believed, to whose troops
received credit for Pickett's Charge (ask a North Carolinian). Sometimes myth
obscures our view of the past—not to mention pride, bias, and emotion—but
more often history itself complicates the picture. However much we'd like to,
we can't know the commanders' minds. We can't always reconcile conflicting
reports. We can't pinpoint locations and times with absolute certainty. Just like
the soldiers, we can't see through the fog of war. We can't know—not truly—what
it was like, all dizzyingly at once, to dash into a stranger's wheat field scores of

miles from home, fire and reload a musket while hundreds of guns blast and hundreds of voices shout and cry and scream, see friends fall in the smoke, and hope like hell to make it back home. But we can try. We must try. Much remains uncertain about this battle and is likely to remain so, but we can keep digging and continue telling—and retelling—the story of Gettysburg.

Throughout his career Don Troiani has tried, has kept digging, and through his art has told some remarkable history. Troiani made his reputation as an artist, but he deserves to be called a historian as well. Like all good historians, Troiani consults a wide array of primary sources: memoirs, letters, diaries, journals, newspapers, after-action reports, quartermaster documents, photographs, and more. He travels to Gettysburg to get the lay of the land, to study fences, boulders, and trees. In a league of his own, he also uses a too-often-overlooked variety of source material—the actual items soldiers wore, carried, and used—and has assembled one of the country's most respected private collections of militaria, from uniforms and saddles to pistols, swords, and cannon. Troiani goes above and beyond to "get it right," for example, firing musket balls into trees and observing the impacts in the bark. Where Shelby Foote or Bruce Catton used carefully wrought metaphors and well-chosen adjectives to turn their research into vivid Civil War history, Troiani relies on colors and shading—the fine artistic craft he has spent decades honing—to do the same, to convey the "wild kaleidoscopic whirl" of Gettysburg.

Long, hot hours after Lee's morning conference on July 2, Longstreet's attack stepped off, and chaotic combat rippled up the battlefield. A Union officer called it "a scene of excitement and confusion and grandeur and horror, as nothing but the simile of hell broke loose is at all adequate to describe." That afternoon's fighting in places such as Devil's Den, Little Round Top, the Wheatfield, and the Peach Orchard captured Don Troiani's imagination, and he has depicted—one is tempted to say *recorded*—the action in a series of paintings in this book. May the great deeds of Gettysburg, seen here through Troiani's art and history, capture your imagination, too.

David Reisch, history editor, Stackpole Books

Introduction

The Battle of Gettysburg

SOMETIME AROUND 7:30 ON THE MORNING OF JULY 1, 1863, SOLDIERS OF the 8th Illinois Cavalry peered west down the Chambersburg Pike outside Gettysburg, Pennsylvania. The men belonged to a vidette, or forward posting, of William Gamble's brigade of John Buford's cavalry division. Off in the distance they could see lines of Confederate soldiers marching toward them. Lt. Marcellus Jones asked Pvt. George Heim if he could borrow his carbine. Jones took the weapon, rested it on the top rail of a fence, aimed at a Rebel soldier riding a light-colored horse, and squeezed the trigger. It was unlikely that the bullet would hit its target at a distance of 600 yards, but nonetheless Jones had fired the first shot of the Battle of Gettysburg.

Or had he? The 9th New York Cavalry claimed the same honor. Cpl. Alpheus Hodge of that regiment, part of Col. Thomas Devin's brigade of Buford's division, claimed he had shot at some Confederates around 5:20 that morning. According to one account, the enemy soldiers fired first. If that was truly the case, then the Confederates should receive credit for the first shot. To further confuse the matter, soldiers of the 17th Pennsylvania Cavalry said they had been skirmishing with Rebels around 6:00 that morning, about ninety minutes before Marcellus Jones borrowed Private Heims's carbine.[1]

The credit for the "first shot" of Gettysburg is just one of many unsettled questions that bedevil the battle's historians. Gettysburg may be the most studied battle in history. Although scores of books and articles have been written about Gettysburg, many topics remain open to argument—and people do argue about them, vehemently and at length, more than a century and a half after the fighting ended. Did Jeb Stuart shirk his duty to embark on a quest for glory before the battle? Should Richard Ewell have attacked Cemetery Hill on July 1? Did James Longstreet drag his feet on July 2? Did Union general Daniel Sickles save the battle for the Union or nearly lose it? Did Union commander George Gordon Meade want to retreat from Gettysburg? Who was the real hero of Little Round Top? Did the Rebels have a chance for victory on July 3, or was Pickett's Charge doomed from the start?

People care so much because those three momentous days in Pennsylvania appear to be a historical pivot point, the "high-water mark of the Confederacy," the turning point of the Civil War. "The issue of the campaign and of the Civil War itself, as history shows, was trembling in the balance," remembered a sergeant in the 7th Virginia. "Victory or defeat to either side would be in effect a settlement of the issues involved; this the officers and men seemed clearly to realize."

THE AMERICAN CIVIL WAR HAD BEEN RAGING FOR SLIGHTLY MORE THAN two years by the time Jones squeezed off his shot. Sectional tensions had reached the breaking point in December 1860 when South Carolina, worried that the incoming Republican administration of president-elect Abraham Lincoln would take steps to end slavery, seceded from the Union. Other Southern states followed, and together they formed the Confederate States of America. The simmering tensions burst into flame on April 12, 1861, when Confederate artillery fired at the Federal Fort Sumter in Charleston Harbor.

That July, Union and Confederate forces met near Manassas, Virginia, in the first major battle of the war. The Rebels gained the victory, but both sides realized the war would be neither short nor bloodless. In the spring of 1862, the Union Army of the Potomac, under Maj. Gen. George B. McClellan, marched up the peninsula between the York and James Rivers and threatened the Confederate capital of Richmond, coming so close its soldiers could hear the city's church bells. But after the defending army's commander, Joseph E. Johnston, was injured at the battle of Seven Pines (Fair Oaks), his army received a new leader.

Gen. Robert E. Lee had been a hero of the Mexican-American War and served as the superintendent of the United States Military Academy at West Point. At the start of the war, Union general-in-chief Winfield Scott had offered Lee command of the Union armies. Instead, Lee had thrown in his lot with the Confederacy. After serving without particular distinction in western Virginia and South Carolina, Lee was in Richmond serving as military advisor to Confederate president Jefferson Davis when Johnston was wounded.

Lee named his new command the Army of Northern Virginia and forced McClellan away from Richmond during the Seven Days' Battle. At the end of August, Lee earned another hard-fought victory when he defeated a cobbled-together Union army under John Pope at Second Bull Run (called Second Manassas in the South). Lee then continued the offensive by taking his army into Maryland. McClellan, back at the head of a reconstituted Army of the Potomac, managed to fight Lee to a draw at the battle of Antietam in September.

Antietam was not a clear-cut victory, but it was close enough for Lincoln, who used the opportunity to issue his preliminary Emancipation Proclamation and announce his intention to free all slaves in Rebel-held territory. It fundamentally changed the course of the war. No longer was the Union fighting strictly to restore the Union. Ending slavery had become a goal as well.

Lincoln grew tired of McClellan's inactivity following Antietam, and in November he replaced him with Ambrose Burnside, a general too willing to admit he neither wanted nor deserved the position. Burnside proved the accuracy of his self-assessment that December at the battle of Fredericksburg, when he sent wave after wave of soldiers against a nearly impregnable Confederate position behind the town. Troubled by the defeat and by the grumblings by the army's generals, Lincoln replaced Burnside with Maj. Gen. Joseph Hooker at the beginning of 1863. At first it seemed a good move. Hooker reinvigorated the army and made plans to strike Lee—still behind the Rappahannock River around Fredericksburg.

Hooker sent his army into motion at the end of April and made a commendable start on a movement to outflank Lee's army. Then he appeared to lose his nerve and settled into a defensive posture as he invited Lee to attack. Lee accepted the invitation with a vengeance, sending Thomas "Stonewall" Jackson on a sweeping flank march to attack Hooker's unsuspecting right flank, held by Maj. Gen. Oliver Otis Howard's XI Corps. Surprised and outnumbered, the XI Corps went reeling back under the onslaught. Tough fighting by the Union troops managed to stabilize things by nightfall—aided by the mortal wounding of Jackson by some of his own soldiers. Nonetheless, after another day of bloody combat, Hooker decided to recross the Rappahannock and return his army to the camps they had left only days before.

Encouraged by the Army of Northern Virginia's continued successes, Lee decided to again bring the war to the North. First, though, he reorganized his army by forming it into three corps. James Longstreet retained command of the I Corps. Born in South Carolina but raised in Georgia, Longstreet had earned his reputation as Lee's "old war horse." Richard Ewell, who had returned to the army after losing a leg at Second Bull Run, replaced Jackson at the head of the II Corps. Ambrose Powell Hill had earned renown as head of his "light division," and he was promoted to take the newly formed III Corps. The flamboyant but immensely capable James Ewell Brown "Jeb" Stuart retained command of the army's cavalry.

Despite its losses at Chancellorsville, the Rebel army was flush with success. Its men had whipped the Yankees before and had little doubt they would do it again. "I am sure there can never have been an army with more supreme confidence in its commander than that army had in Gen. Lee," said Edward Porter Alexander, who commanded artillery in Longstreet's corps. "We looked forward to victory under him as confidently as to successive sunrises."[2]

The Army of the Potomac had fewer reasons for confidence, but its command structure remained relatively intact. Alfred Pleasonton replaced George Stoneman as head of the cavalry, and II Corps commander Darius Couch refused to serve any longer under Hooker, so he was sent to Harrisburg, Pennsylvania, to head the military department there. Maj. Gen. Winfield Scott Hancock, a Pennsylvanian whom McClellan had dubbed "the Superb" after his performance on the Peninsula, replaced Couch. John Reynolds, another dependable Pennsylvanian, remained in command of the I Corps. Daniel Sickles, a New York politician who had gained notoriety as a congressman when he killed his wife's lover in Washington before the war, led the III Corps. The V Corps' commander was George Gordon Meade, another Pennsylvanian. He had been badly wounded on the Peninsula but returned in time to fight at Second Bull Run. Some of his fellow generals were talking about the possibility of Meade replacing Hooker.

Connecticut native Maj. Gen. John Sedgwick commanded the VI Corps. He was a solid, if perhaps overly cautious, commander. Maine native Oliver Otis Howard remained in command of the XI Corps, despite his poor performance at Chancellorsville. He hoped for a chance to redeem himself. New Yorker Henry Slocum led the XII Corps.

On June 3, Lee began moving his army from its camps around Fredericksburg for the start of what would become the Gettysburg campaign. His objective was to move his army north, down the Shenandoah Valley, screened from prying Union eyes by the Blue Ridge Mountains. Ewell and the II Corps departed first, followed by Longstreet. Hill and the III Corps remained for a time around Fredericksburg to hold the Union army in place.

Before embarking on the campaign, cavalry leader Jeb Stuart indulged his love of pageantry by holding a grand review of his command near Brandy Station, a stop on the Orange & Alexandria Railroad. When Hooker received intelligence about the gathering, he dispatched Pleasonton's cavalry, supported by a couple of infantry brigades, to disrupt things. The result was the battle of Brandy Station, North America's largest cavalry battle. More than 20,000 soldiers, including the two brigades of Union infantry, fought for the better part of the day on June 9 before Pleasonton withdrew his forces. The Union did not score a victory, but the battle served notice that the Federal cavalry had become a force to be reckoned with.

After Brandy Station, the two cavalries crossed and recrossed sabers in a series of battles on the edge of the Shenandoah Valley, at Aldie, Middletown, and Upperville. His job of blocking the Union cavalry finished, Stuart and his best three brigades set off on June 25 on what would become one of the most controversial actions of the Gettysburg campaign. Stuart's ride around the Union army left him out of contact with Lee until July 2. Some accuse Stuart of attempting to burnish his reputation after the humiliation of Brandy Station. Others fault Lee for issuing vague and sometimes contradictory orders, and for not properly utilizing the cavalry brigades Stuart left behind. What cannot be denied is that Jeb Stuart remained out of contact with his army commander until he showed up at Lee's headquarters on Gettysburg's second day.

Lee's army continued its movement north without Stuart. Ewell's corps captured Winchester, and the Union soldiers who were not killed or taken prisoner fled north. The Army of Northern Virginia followed into Maryland and Pennsylvania. Ewell's men radiated out across central Pennsylvania, with division commander Jubal Early overseeing the capture of York and sending John B. Gordon's brigade to Wrightsville on the Susquehanna River. Ewell was with the divisions of Robert Rodes and Edward Johnson in Carlisle. Albert Jenkins's cavalry moved even further north to capture Mechanicsburg. Jenkins even scouted the defenses of Harrisburg to see if the state capital was ripe for the plucking.

On June 28, the Army of the Potomac received a new commander. Hooker had gotten into a spat with general-in-chief Henry Halleck over control of the Union garrison at Harpers Ferry. Hooker offered his resignation; Lincoln and Halleck accepted it. They replaced him with George Meade, who accepted the assignment with reluctance. "Well, I have been tried and condemned without a hearing, and I suppose I will have to go to the execution," Meade grumbled to the messenger who brought him his orders outside Frederick, Maryland.

By June 30 Meade had moved his headquarters to Taneytown, Maryland. He had his engineers survey the nearby terrain to find a suitable defensive position should Lee move south and attack. They selected a line behind Big Pipe Creek that offered excellent defensive possibilities, was close to the army's supply lines, and would keep the Army of the Potomac between the Rebel army and Washington and Baltimore. On the morning of July 1 Meade issued his "Pipe Creek Circular," in which he outlined plans to draw Lee south to attack the Pipe Creek line. He also noted, "Developments may cause the commanding general to assume the offensive from his present position." Developments caused him to do exactly that, but Meade's critics later used the circular as evidence that the general would have preferred to retreat from Gettysburg.

On the day that Meade assumed command of the army, Lee was in Chambersburg, Pennsylvania. He had expected Stuart to inform him when the Army of the Potomac crossed its namesake river. Instead, he received that information on June 28 from a spy working for Longstreet. Lee sent out messengers to call back his scattered army to the area of Cashtown, Pennsylvania, on the eastern side of South Mountain. Once Lee's subordinates received their orders, the gray tide began to recede from central Pennsylvania and concentrate in Adams County. The county seat was a town called Gettysburg, the center of a converging network of roads that made it a natural meeting point for armies on the march through Pennsylvania.

July 1, 1863

THE SOLDIERS THAT THE 8TH ILLINOIS CAVALRY SAW ON THE CHAMBERSBURG Pike on July 1 belonged to the division of Henry Heth, from A. P. Hill's III Corps. Heth (pronounced Heath) had at least two marks of distinction—he was supposedly the only Confederate officer whom Robert E. Lee addressed by his first name, and he had come in dead last in the West Point class of 1847. Heth and Hill both knew that Lee did not want to bring on a general engagement until his entire army was up, but Heth ended up doing that anyway. Heth later said he asked Hill if he could take his men into Gettysburg because he had heard there were shoes to be had in town. It seems unlikely that footwear motivated Heth's actions—but they might have provided a handy excuse for recklessly precipitating a battle despite Lee's orders.

On the morning of July 1, 1863, Heth's division began their fateful march down the Chambersburg Pike, where John Buford and his cavalry were waiting. Buford, a tough and capable Kentuckian, had reached Gettysburg on June 30 and was growing increasingly anxious over his scouts' reports about approaching Rebels. When one of his brigade commanders declared his confidence that the cavalry could hold the Rebels back until the infantry arrived, Buford corrected him. "You will have to fight like the devil to hold your own until supports arrive," Buford said.

It was an accurate prediction.

Buford's two brigades of cavalry fought a tenacious but increasingly desperate delaying action against Heth's division. A battery of horse artillery, under the command of John Calef and attached to William Gamble's brigade, came clattering up and was soon dueling with Confederate artillery. (The gun that fired Calef's first shot is one of four Union cannon at the base of Buford's statue on the Chambersburg Pike.) "The enemy's infantry advanced rapidly, and the musketry and artillery fire soon became extremely warm," Calef said.[3]

Buford knew that help was coming when John Reynolds reached the field around ten o'clock that morning. Meade had put his fellow Pennsylvanian in command of the left wing of the army, which included Reynolds's own I Corps, Howard's XI, and Sickles's III. The I Corps was not far behind Reynolds. There are conflicting accounts of the meeting between Buford and Reynolds. Buford's signal officer said Reynolds found Buford at the Lutheran Seminary on the ridge west of town that bore its name. "What's the problem, John?" Reynolds called up to Buford, who was surveying the fight from the seminary's cupola. "The devil's to pay!" replied Buford. This version of the meeting is "dear to the heart of the romanticists," opined historian Coddington, but other accounts place the meeting further west, on another slight rise called McPherson Ridge. No matter where they met or what they said, there can be little doubt that Buford communicated the seriousness of the situation.[4]

Lysander Cutler's brigade of the I Corps was the first Union infantry to arrive. It moved north of the pike, where Cutler later gave one of his regiments, the 56th Pennsylvania, credit for firing the first volley at Gettysburg. This has been disputed, with the 2nd Wisconsin of the Iron Brigade also claiming the distinction. "Questions about who fired the first shot or what unit arrived first were taken very seriously by Civil War veterans and became the occasion for debates, some of them quite acrimonious," noted Coddington.[5]

Reynolds also ordered up Capt. James Hall's 2nd Maine Battery and posted it in an exposed position on the pike. Reynolds promised Hall that Cutler would provide infantry support, and then rode off to guide other units of the I Corps into position.

One of those units was the 1st brigade of the 1st division in the I Corps. Known as the Iron Brigade, it was the only Western brigade in the Army of the Potomac, with regiments from Indiana (the 19th), Michigan (the 24th), and Wisconsin (the 2nd, 6th, and 7th). It had earned its nickname while under the command of John Gibbon during the Antietam campaign and was recognizable by the tall, black Hardee hats many of its men wore. Now commanded by Gen. Solomon "Long Sol" Meredith, who stood a towering 6 feet 7 inches, the brigade reached the field in the nick of time. Reynolds waved them into position through some woods and toward the banks of Willoughby Run. "Forward men, forward for God's sake, and drive those fellows out of the woods," the general commanded. As he wheeled in his saddle to look for the troops approaching behind him, a bullet slammed into the back of his neck. Reynolds fell from his horse and died almost instantly.

The Iron Brigade swarmed into Herbst Woods and across Willoughby Run, where they crashed into the Alabamians and Tennesseans of Brig. Gen. James Archer's brigade. During the fighting, Pvt. Patrick Maloney of the 2nd Wisconsin spotted Archer, charged up to him, and demanded his surrender. "It is to be regretted that this brave Irishman was subsequently killed in the action," reported I Corps commander Abner Doubleday.[6]

Things were not going as well for the Union north of the Chambersburg Pike, where Brig. Gen. Joseph Davis's three Mississippi brigades and one North Carolina brigade advanced west from Herr's Ridge toward Cutler's brigade on McPherson Ridge. Cutler's men fell back, forcing Hall's 2nd Maine Battery to follow suit. "You may judge when I tell you that many of our horses were not shot but *bayoneted* that it was a close and *desperate struggle* for our guns two of which they actually had hold of at one time," Hall wrote to Maine's adjutant general.[7]

Davis's men had tilted the battle in the Rebels' favor, but only briefly. Three regiments, the 6th Wisconsin of the Iron Brigade and the 84th and 95th New York, counterattacked from south of the pike. Some of the Confederates then made the fatal mistake of taking cover inside a deep, unfinished railroad cut. It must have looked like an ideal defensive position, but it turned out to be a trap. Union soldiers appeared on the rim, muskets pointed at the Rebels below them. "Throw down your muskets! Down with your muskets!" the Union soldiers called. "The coolness, self-possession, and discipline which held back our men from pouring in a general volley saved a hundred lives on the enemy," remembered Col. Rufus Dawes of the 6th Wisconsin.[8]

It was now around noon. A comparative quiet fell over the battlefield as both sides took time to regroup and lick their wounds.

WHEN THE FIGHTING RESUMED AROUND 2:30 THAT AFTERNOON, THE Army of the Potomac faced a new threat. Robert Rodes's division, from Ewell's II Corps, had arrived from the north to take a position on Oak Hill, a prominent rise northwest of Gettysburg. Rodes was in a perfect position to hit the I Corps with enfilading artillery fire. His initial infantry assaults, however, were not so successful. Col. Edward O'Neal's brigade made a disorganized attack against Henry Baxter's brigade on Oak Ridge on the far right of the I Corps. "After a desperate fight of about fifteen minutes, we were compelled to fall back," recalled one Alabamian. Brig. Gen. Alfred Iverson's brigade met with disaster when it made a rash advance toward Baxter's men, who remained hidden behind a stone wall until the Confederates were within killing distance. "A sheet of fire and smoke belched from the wall, flashing full in the faces of the Confederates," a Union soldier wrote. The volley was so deadly that many of Iverson's men fell where they stood, in lines as neat as though they were on parade.[9]

Despite the twin repulses, Rodes managed to regroup and send his brigades forward again. He had not only the I Corps to deal with, but also the Union XI Corps, which had come streaming out from Gettysburg's northern outskirts into the flat plain below Oak Hill.

The XI Corps had been commanded by Oliver Otis Howard, who was still smarting from the debacle of Chancellorsville. Following Reynolds's death, Howard became the Union's ranking officer on the field, so he ceded command of the corps to Maj. Gen. Carl Schurz. Probably Howard's most important decision was to post Adolph von Steinwehr's division in reserve on the dominating heights of Cemetery Hill, the site of the town's Evergreen Cemetery south of town. It sat at the northern end of a low ridgeline called Cemetery Ridge, which ran south to a pair of small hills—Big Round Top and Little Round Top.

There has been debate over whether or not Howard should have cut his losses and moved the I Corps back toward town instead of sending the XI out in a futile attempt to align on its right. The two corps never did meet up. Instead, there was a gap between their lines that separated at an almost ninety-degree angle. Making matters worse, XI Corps division commander Francis Barlow decided to move his men forward to a slight rise on his front, known today as Barlow's Knoll. This extended the line, weakening it further.

Timing could not have been better for Lee or worse for the Army of the Potomac. John Gordon's brigade of Early's division splashed across Rock Creek and slammed into Barlow's exposed line even as the Georgians of George Doles's brigade in Rodes's division hit it from the left. The XI Corps soldiers did what they could—a Georgia soldier said the Federals had "stood firm" at first, and when they did retreat they "were harder to drive than we had ever known them before"—but it was a doomed effort. They began to fall back into the town.[10]

Barlow fell badly wounded during the fight with Gordon's brigade. Gordon's account of meeting the apparently dying general on the battlefield, and their encounter in Washington after the war, became a widely told story, although there are doubts about its veracity. "Although it is a good story, Gordon probably embellished the battlefield meeting, if it occurred at all," noted Christian G. Samito, who edited Barlow's letters.[11]

Historian Harry Pfanz says that Lee's movements on July 1 "seem impossible to reconstruct," but it appears he reached the battlefield by 2:00 P.M., still unwilling to fight a general engagement until his entire army had arrived. At some point he must have changed his mind, for Harry Heth received orders to renew the fight he had started that morning. Heth resumed his push forward, now bolstered by brigades under James Pettigrew (who took on division command when Heth was wounded) and John Brockenbrough.

Pettigrew's brigade began its advance around 2:30. One of its regiments was the 26th North Carolina, under its "boy colonel," twenty-one-year-old Henry K. Burgwyn, who had been born in his mother's native state of Massachusetts but grew up in his father's North Carolina. During the fight against the Iron Brigade's 24th Michigan on the banks of Willoughby Run, the 26th North Carolina's flag fell to the ground when the latest in a series of color bearers went down. Burgwyn retrieved the flag and had just handed it off to yet another color bearer when a minié ball knocked him to the ground, mortally wounded.

Dorsey Pender's division of Hill's 3rd Corps added its weight to the push against the I Corps on McPherson Ridge, stretching to the right of Heth's men and extending far to the left of the Union line. To the north, a portion of Junius Daniels's brigade of Rodes's division hit Roy Stone's brigade of the Pennsylvania Bucktails around the barn and buildings of the McPherson farm. Under such unrelenting pressure from two sides, the Union troops were forced to give way and retreat eastward to Seminary Ridge. There was more furious fighting around the Lutheran Seminary, but when the South Carolinians of Abner Perrin's brigade smashed into the left of the I Corps, the Union soldiers retreated into town toward the high ground of Cemetery Hill.

The 16th Maine, part of Gabriel Paul's brigade of John Robinson's division, was on the far right of the I Corps. Robinson—"the hairiest general I ever saw," in the opinion of one Maine soldier—selected the 16th Maine to buy his division some time. He ordered Col. Charles Tilden to hold a forward position "at any cost." Tilden did as he was ordered, and his men made a doomed stand against the advancing Rebels of Rodes's division. When they were about to be overwhelmed, the Maine soldiers tore up their flags and distributed the pieces so the banners wouldn't be captured. Of the 275 men from the regiment who had reached Gettysburg on July 1, the adjutant counted only 35 who made it back to Cemetery Hill.

Howard's decision to post a reserve on the hill proved valuable indeed, and the defeated Federals began converting the rise into a strong position. Howard, however, was "mortified" when Winfield Scott Hancock reached the battlefield with orders from Meade to take charge, even though Howard outranked him. But Hancock had Meade's confidence, and he possessed a natural air of command that stiffened the backbone of the Union troops. Howard's bruised feelings notwithstanding, the two generals managed to work side-by-side and organize a defense against the impending Confederate attack.

The attack did not come that evening, and the reasons why have become among the most contested issues of the battle. As the Union forces fell back through town to the heights that Howard had selected to the south, Lee—now willing to take advantage of his army's gains—sent Richard Ewell a message telling him to capture Cemetery Hill "if practicable."

Ewell, known as "Old Bald Head," had performed well on the campaign so far, and his men had already done plenty of hard marching and fighting on July 1. Furthermore, one of his divisions—under Maj. Gen. Edward Johnson—had not reached the field, and two brigades—Brig. Gen. William Smith's and Gordon's—were to the north responding to false alarms about Yankees approaching from the rear. Under those circumstances, and facing a rapidly strengthening Federal position, Ewell decided that an attack was not, in fact, practicable. His decision sparked a controversy that endures today. By not striking when the iron was hot, his detractors maintain, Ewell lost the battle and therefore the war. However, as historian Gary Gallagher noted, the critics often "minimized the obstacles faced by Ewell and exaggerated the Second Corps chief's indecision." Lee's soldiers would have to be satisfied with what they had gained already.[12]

July 2, 1863

GEORGE MEADE REACHED THE BATTLEFIELD FROM HIS HEADQUARTERS IN TANEY-town sometime in the early hours of July 2. He met corps commanders Slocum, Howard, and Sickles on Cemetery Hill. They told Meade that the army had a good defensive position. "I am glad to hear you say so, gentlemen," Meade said, "for it is too late to leave it."

Sickles was not feeling so sanguine later that morning. He claimed he did not know exactly where Meade wanted him to place his III Corps, even though Meade's instructions seemed fairly straightforward—Sickles was to connect to the right of the II Corps on Cemetery Ridge and extend the line in the direction of the two low hills—Big Round Top and Little Round Top—to his left. The III Corps would have completed what has become known as the Union's "fishhook," a line that started on the right at Culp's Hill, curved around Cemetery Hill, and continued south down Cemetery Ridge. This offered the advantage of interior lines, meaning Meade could shift troops from one end to the other fairly easily. In contrast, Lee's much longer exterior lines, wrapping around the outside of the fishhook, made communication more difficult.

But Sickles fretted. The portion of Cemetery Ridge he was supposed to occupy petered out into a swampy lowland that offered few obvious advantages. He wanted to move forward to higher ground in front of him, including a peach orchard owned by farmer Joseph Sherfy. When Sickles's objections reached Meade, the army commander sent artillery chief Henry Hunt to III Corps headquarters. Hunt could see some advantages to the line Sickles preferred, but saw disadvantages, too. It would have been a much longer position to defend, and Sickles did not have enough troops. The proposed line would also bend at the peach orchard, creating an exposed salient. Sickles asked Hunt if he could move forward. "Not on my authority; I will report to General Meade for his instructions," Hunt replied.[13]

Sickles became even more perturbed later in the day when soldiers of the 3rd Maine supported Hiram Berdan's sharpshooters in a skirmish in woods on the other side of the Emmitsburg Road. Sickles became convinced the Rebels were about to fall on his left, and he decided he had to do something about it. He ordered his corps forward. Andrew Humphreys's division advanced all the way to the Emmitsburg Road, a good half-mile west of Cemetery Ridge. From there his line tailed off southeast to the Peach Orchard. David Birney's division continued the line through a wheat field, across Houck's Ridge, and to a place of jumbled boulders in front of Little Round Top called Devil's Den.

When Meade heard about the surprise move, he galloped out to the Peach Orchard to find Sickles. Meade had a fiery temper, especially when under stress, and he no doubt expressed himself strongly. Sickles offered to move back to his original line, but Meade told him it was too late. He promised to send whatever support he could when the Rebels attacked.

Sickles's occupation of the Peach Orchard turned out to be a surprise for the Army of Northern Virginia as well, on a day plagued by missteps and poor intelligence. Lee's troubles started with a faulty reconnaissance of the Union lines. On the morning of July 2, Lee sent a party under Capt. Samuel Johnston to reconnoiter the Union left. Johnston departed around four o'clock that morning. When he reported to Lee about three hours later, Johnston said he had gone all the way to the slopes of Little Round Top and had not seen any Union troops nearby. How Johnston could have missed the soldiers just north of the hill remains a mystery, but his report gave Lee the mistaken impression that the Union line did not extend as far as it did and that its left flank was "up in the air."

Lee based his plans on this flawed assumption. He wanted Longstreet to move to the south with his two divisions (Pickett's had not reached the field) and attack the Union left by moving north up the Emmitsburg Road. It appears he was under the impression that this would strike the unsuspecting Union flank, which he apparently believed was on the road near the Codori farm. After Longstreet began his attack, units of A. P. Hill's corps would extend the fight to the north, and Ewell would press an attack on the Union right.

Longstreet argued against making the attack at all. After the war, Longstreet wrote that Lee had agreed to make the Pennsylvania campaign "offensive in strategy but defensive in tactics, forcing the Federal army to give us battle when we were in a strong position and ready to receive them." Or so he said. Many doubt that the aggressive Lee would have been so willing to let a subordinate dictate his plans that way. In any event, Longstreet said he suggested that Lee move the entire army in a wide flanking movement and place it between Meade and Washington and Baltimore so the Federals would have to take the offensive. Lee was having none of it. "No," he said, "the enemy is there, and I am going to attack him there." Lee remained insistent that Longstreet attack north up the Emmitsburg Road and crush the Union left.[14]

Longstreet reluctantly set out with his divisions, but poor scouting led to problems and delays. The route Longstreet intended to take would have exposed his columns to Union signalmen on Little Round Top. To keep out of sight, Longstreet had to reverse course and make a lengthy countermarch to find a new trail. Much valuable time was lost.

It wasn't until sometime around four o'clock that Longstreet was on Warfield Ridge, ready to unleash his assault on the Union left, wherever that might be. Much to Longstreet's surprise, he found a strong force of Union artillery and infantry occupying a peach orchard along the Emmitsburg Road to the north—part of Dan Sickles's III Corps. Seemingly resentful that Lee had disregarded his advice, Longstreet refused to listen to his subordinates' pleas to alter the battle plan. Division commander John Bell Hood wanted to target the two large hills—the Round Tops—to his front. "General Lee's orders are to attack up the Emmitsburg Road," Longstreet responded. Maybe he was being sulky. Maybe he was simply following orders.

In any event, the attack did not move north up the Emmitsburg Road. When Evander Law and his brigade of Alabamians from Hood's division led the attack, they immediately moved east of the Emmitsburg Road and toward the Round Tops. Hood's other brigade, Jerome Robertson's four Texas regiments and the 3rd Arkansas, initially tried to keep its left on the road, but that would have opened a gap between his brigade and Law's. Lee's plan was unraveling from the start.

Defending Houk's Ridge and Devil's Den were regiments of Hobart Ward's brigade of David Birney's III Corps division. Arrayed above the den and along the ridge were four guns of James Smith's 4th New York Independent Battery. Smith did not have room to place all six of his guns there, so he put the final two to his right rear in the Plum Run Valley.

Smith's gun crews were soon firing at the Confederates moving from Warfield Ridge. "I never saw the men do better work; every shot told; the pieces were discharged as rapidly as they could be with regard to effectiveness, while the conduct of the men was superb," Smith said. But the soldiers from Texas and Arkansas could take advantage of the rough terrain to find cover. Rebel sharpshooters began to take a toll on the Union artillery. When the Confederates approached through a triangle-shaped field below Smith's guns, the cannoneers could no longer lower the gun barrels enough to provide effective fire.[15]

To Smith's right, Col. Van Horne Ellis and Maj. James Cromwell of the 124th New York—the "Orange Blossoms"—watched the approaching Confederates from horseback, presenting ideal targets for enemy sharpshooters. An aide suggested that the officers dismount. Ellis refused. "The men must see us now," he said. The Rebels continued their advance, and Ellis ordered a charge. The New Yorkers initially drove the 1st Texas back, but Cromwell and Ellis both fell dead in the fight and the Federals had to retreat.

As the Texas and Arkansas troops made their frontal attack on Devil's Den, two Alabama regiments that Law had sent swinging around behind his brigade attacked the Plum Run Valley from the south. Brig. Gen. Henry Benning's brigade of Georgians, following behind the Texans, also added their weight to the assault. Smith was running low on ammunition and getting desperate. "For God's sake, men, don't let them take my guns away from me," he implored the survivors of the 124th New York. His pleading was in vain, and the Rebels swept the Union defenders from Devil's Den and captured three of Smith's guns in the process. Little Round Top lay just ahead of them.[16]

On the afternoon of July 2, Maj. Gen. Gouverneur Warren, a New Yorker who served as Meade's chief engineer, was dismayed to learn that the only Union soldiers on Little Round Top belonged to the signal corps. Warren dispatched a messenger to V Corps commander George Sykes to ask for troops. Sykes, in response, sent a message to division commander James Barnes. The messenger did not find Barnes. Instead, he found Col. Strong Vincent, one of his brigade commanders. On his own authority, Vincent took his brigade to defend the rocky hill.

Vincent positioned his men on the southern slope of Little Round Top, a rocky spur that descended into a little wooded valley before the land rose to ascend Big Round Top. Brandishing his wife's riding crop, Vincent hastily placed his four regiments. The 20th Maine, under Bowdoin College professor Joshua Lawrence Chamberlain, was on the far left. Next came Vincent's old command, the 83rd Pennsylvania, then the 44th New York and the 16th Michigan. The 20th Maine was now the left of the entire Union army, and Vincent ordered its newly promoted colonel, who had yet to command the regiment in battle, to hold his position "at all costs."

Vincent's men had hardly shuffled into line before the attack came. Alabamians from Laws's brigade—the 15th and 47th Alabama—appeared out of the woods to their front. The 15th was led by Col. William Oates, and the 47th by Lt. Col. Michael Bulger. Both regiments had already had a trying day. They had marched twenty-four miles just to reach the battlefield before stepping off from Warfield Ridge to attack the Union lines. The men Oates had sent to fill canteens for his regiment had been captured, so the Alabama soldiers were parched. Union sharpshooters had harassed them, so the tired and thirsty Rebels had pursued them up all the way to the top of Big Round Top before Oates received orders to climb back down the hill and attack the Union soldiers forming on the smaller hill to the north.

The 47th Alabama hit the right of the 20th Maine and the left of the 83rd Pennsylvania. The 15th Alabama concentrated on the left of the 20th Maine, and Oates attempted to flank the Maine men. Chamberlain responded by stretching out his line and "refusing" his flank by bending his formation into a V. Again and again the Alabamians attempted to break that line. Again and again the Maine soldiers stopped them. "There were never harder fighters than the Twentieth Maine men and their gallant Colonel," Oates recalled years later. Oates's own brother was mortally wounded during the fight.[17]

Someone had to give, and in the end the Alabamians did. Chamberlain recalled that his regiment's ammunition was running low. He was not sure if the 20th Maine could resist another attack. "I saw that the *defensive* could be maintained not an instant longer, & with a few gallant officers rallied a line, ordered 'bayonets fixed,' & 'forward' *at a run*," Chamberlain reported. The men of the 20th Maine, bayonets lowered, made their mad, desperate charge down the southern spur of Little Round Top, and the exhausted, battered survivors of the 15th Alabama broke and ran.[18]

Like so much about Gettysburg, the final bayonet charge of the 20th Maine has been studied, interpreted, and argued over. Did Chamberlain really order it? Wasn't the 15th Alabama already starting to fall back even before the 20th Maine charged down the hill? "It is not believed to be possible to reconcile all the theories and beliefs of the actors, even in so small a space as the front of a regiment," the regiment's historian concluded, "and when we fail, as sometimes we must, we must conclude, that as there is a substantial agreement on the main features of the action, these disputed details were seen from different points, or were viewed at different stages as part of a whole."[19]

Even as the 20th Maine fought on Little Round Top's southern slope, the 4th and 5th Texas from Robertson's brigade assaulted the hill's western face. "Every tree, rock and stump that gave any protection from the rain of minie-balls, that was poured down upon us, from the crests above us, were soon appropriated," said a soldier from the 4th Texas. "By this time order and discipline were gone. Every fellow was his own general."[20]

The Union defenders beat back the Texans, but, reinforced by the 48th Alabama of Laws's brigade, the Rebels began another attack amid a tumult of shot and shell that "created a scene of such indescribable, awe-inspiring confusion," in the words of one Texan. Under the onslaught, part of the 16th Michigan, Strong Vincent's rightmost regiment, gave way. Vincent jumped atop a rock to encourage his men when a bullet struck him in the groin. Vincent was later promoted to brigadier general as he lay dying in a farmhouse behind Little Round Top.

Gouverneur Warren remained unaware that Vincent's brigade was fighting on the hill's southern end. Desperate to find men to defend what he considered "the key of the whole position," he jumped on a horse to look for them. The first regiment he encountered was the 140th New York, part of Stephen Weed's V Corps brigade. Its colonel was a young Irish immigrant named Patrick O'Rorke. Warren, who had once commanded this very brigade, knew O'Rorke well. "Paddy, give me a regiment," Warren implored, and O'Rorke led his men to the summit of Little Round Top. Once there, he began to get them into formation. Warren told him there was no time for that—the Rebels were about to reach the crest.

"O'Rorke shouted, 'Down this way, boys!'" one of his men recalled, "and following him we rushed down the rocky slope with all the same moral effect upon the rebels, who saw us coming, as if our bayonets had been fixed and we ready to charge upon them. Coming abreast of Vincent's brigade, and taking advantage of such shelter as the huge rocks lying about there afforded, the men loaded and fired, and in less time than it takes to write it the onslaught of the rebels was fairly checked, and in a few minutes the woods in front of us were cleared except of the dead and wounded." One of those dead was O'Rorke, felled by a bullet to the neck in the opening moments of the charge. The arrival of O'Rorke's men was the last straw for the embattled Confederates. They fell back, leaving Little Round Top the property of its Union defenders.[21]

Little Round Top wasn't solely the province of signalmen and artillery. The Union's Battery D, 5th United States Artillery, under Lt. Charles Hazlett, somehow managed to wrestle its heavy 10-pound Parrots up the east side of the hill to the summit, "each man and horse trying to pull the whole battery up by himself," as Lt. Benjamin Franklin Rittenhouse recalled it. Warren remembered agreeing with Hazlett that the narrow and rocky summit "was no place for artillery fire," but both men realized that the thunder of the guns would be reassuring to the defenders. (Confederates also testified to the guns' effect, especially when they began tearing holes through the lines of the Confederates in Pickett's Charge on July 3.) Hazlett was mortally wounded on Little Round Top during the fighting on July 2. According to some accounts, he was shot and killed as he leaned over to hear the dying words of wounded brigade commander Stephen Weed.[22]

Some of the hardest fighting on July 2 took place in George Rose's twenty-six-acre wheat field, east of the Emmitsburg Road. There was a rise at the northeast side of the field where Capt. George E. Wilson posted the six guns of his 1st New York Light Artillery. Another wooded prominence nearby became known as the Stony Hill. A stone fence ran across the south side of the field on the edge of the woods. Under ordinary circumstances this would have been just an ordinary piece of Pennsylvania countryside. But on July 2, 1863, Rose's Wheatfield was destined to becoming a whirlpool of combat, drawing more and more combatants into its maw as the fighting ebbed and flowed, shifting first one way then the other. By the time the fighting was over, the little wheat field had changed hands six times.

George T. Anderson's brigade of Georgians, part of Hood's division, were the first Rebels to arrive. They were halted by Regis De Trobriand's III Corps brigade, including the 17th Maine, which crouched behind a stone wall at the field's southern end. It was "a breast-work ready made," as one of the Maine soldiers recalled, and they used it to help stop the Georgians.

Meade kept his promise to Sickles to provide what troops he could, and he dispatched two brigades of the V Corps—under William Tilton and Jacob Sweitzer—to the Wheatfield to support De Trobriand. Anderson's Rebels received support from South Carolinians of Joseph Kershaw's brigade, who became engaged in a bloody duel with the two V Corps brigades on Stony Hill. Worried that his brigades would be outflanked, James Barnes ordered them to fall back. Kershaw's South Carolinians, with the Georgians of Paul Semmes's brigade behind them, advanced into the Wheatfield.

More Union soldiers stormed into the fray to meet this new threat. These were from John Caldwell's II Corps division, three brigades under Edward Cross, Samuel Zook, and Patrick Kelly, with John Brooke's brigade in reserve. Before marching to the Wheatfield, Kelly's unit, the five war-battered regiments of the Irish Brigade, received absolution from Father William Corby. "The scene was more than impressive, it was awe inspiring," remembered one Irish brigade soldier.[23]

Cross, a no-nonsense New Hampshireman who had experienced a strong presentiment of his own death, fell mortally wounded in the Wheatfield. As he led his men into battle, Zook was also killed. But the Union reinforcements were able to push the Confederates back, and the scales of battle once again appeared to be tilting in the Union's favor. But then the Georgia soldiers of William T. Wofford's brigade entered the fight and shifted the momentum in the other direction.

The experiences of the 4th Michigan show how intense the fighting became. The regiment belonged to Sweitzer's V Corps brigade, which returned to the Wheatfield after its initial withdrawal. During the ensuing struggle with Wofford's men, Rebels grabbed the 4th Michigan's colors. The regiment's colonel, Harrison H. Jeffords, and two other soldiers—one of them Jeffords's brother—made a lunge for the flag. Color bearer Henry S. Seage recalled, "The Colonel secured the colors or at least had his hand on the staff, and in the act of fighting their way out, Col. Jeffords was killed, by bayonet thrust through the body." The other two soldiers were wounded, but the colors of the 4th Michigan were saved.[24]

With the Rebels on his flanks and rear, Sweitzer had no choice but to fight his way out of the Wheatfield to safety. "It is difficult to conceive of a more trying situation than that in which three regiments of this command had lately found themselves, and from which they had just effected their escape," said Sweitzer in his official report. "In fact, I have since understood that one of General Barnes' aides remarked to him shortly after we had advanced, when it was discovered the enemy was behind us on the flank, that he might bid good-bye to the Second Brigade."[25] With the Wheatfield in their hands, the Confederates began to move toward the base of Little Round Top. It was time for the Pennsylvania Reserves division to enter the fight.

The two brigades, under division commander Brig. Gen. Samuel Crawford, had just joined the Army of the Potomac in Frederick on June 28, after serving in Washington's defenses. Crawford was a Pennsylvanian who had started his war at Fort Sumter, where he had been an army surgeon. His two brigades at Gettysburg were commanded by Col. Joseph Fisher and Col. William McCandless.

With Fisher's brigade dispatched to the crest of Little Round Top, the men of McCandless's brigade watched as the Rebels pushed through the Wheatfield and in the direction of Little Round Top. "Not a moment was to be lost," Crawford reported. "Uncovering our front, I ordered an immediate advance. The command advanced gallantly with loud cheers. Two well-directed volleys were delivered upon the advancing masses of the enemy, when the whole column charged at a run down the slope, driving the enemy back across the space beyond and across the stone wall, for the possession of which there was a short but determined struggle. The enemy retired to the wheat-field and the woods." Crawford grabbed the flag of the 1st Pennsylvania Reserves and held it as he rode forward. The color bearer, unwilling to part from the colors, reportedly clutched at Crawford's leg and advanced with him. The timely arrival of the Pennsylvanians halted the Confederates.[26]

Meanwhile, the Mississippians of William Barksdale's brigade of Lafayette McLaws's I Corps division had been cutting a swathe through the soldiers of the Union III Corps. Barksdale, a former congressman and an ardent secessionist, had been straining at the leash to enter the fight as he waited for his orders to advance. When McLaws ordered them forward, Barksdale and his men attacked with a fury. They drove the Union defenders from Sherfy's Peach Orchard—capturing III Corps brigade commander Charles Graham as they did so—and wreaked continued havoc among the III Corps soldiers and batteries as they advanced.

One of those batteries was John Bigelow's 9th Massachusetts, which was receiving its combat baptism. When Barksdale's men approached the battery's position along the Wheatfield Road, Bigelow had to withdraw "by prolongue," meaning his men dragged the guns off by hand, using the guns' recoil to help. They made it as far as the brick Trostle barn, and Lt. Col. Freeman McGilvery found Bigelow there. McGilvery, a former sea captain from Maine, commanded a brigade in the artillery reserve. Late on the afternoon on July 2, he realized that Caldwell's departure for the Wheatfield had created a great gap in the Union line on Cemetery Ridge. With no infantry available to plug the hole, McGilvery decided he would do it with artillery, and he set out to cobble together enough guns to hold the Rebels until infantry support could arrive.

"The crisis of the engagement had now arrived," McGilvery reported. "I gave Captain Bigelow orders to hold his position as long as possible at all hazards, in order to give me time to form a new line of artillery, and justice demands that I should state Captain Bigelow did hold his position and execute his firing with a deliberation and destructive effect upon the enemy in a manner such as only a brave and skillful officer could, until—one officer killed and the others wounded, and more than half his men either killed or wounded, and his horses all shot down at the limbers—he was forced to leave four guns and retire." Bigelow's bugler helped the wounded officer to the rear. He left four guns behind and lost forty-five horses and twenty-eight men.[27]

McGilvery had done well, too. "I feel it due to bring to the notice of the commanding general the intrepid conduct and excellent judgment displayed by Maj. F. McGilvery, First Maine Artillery, under whose immediate command fell many of the reserve batteries engaged on our left center," noted Brig. Gen. R. O. Tyler, commander of the artillery reserve.

The 21st Mississippi captured Bigelow's guns, but the forward momentum of Barksdale's brigade was finally stalling. Yet another unit pulled from Cemetery Ridge—Col. George Willard's brigade of New Yorkers from Alexander Hays's II Corps division—arrived in time to finally check the Mississippians' seemingly inexorable advance. Willard's men had been taunted as "Harpers Ferry cowards" after being captured earlier in the war, but they proved their mettle at Gettysburg. Amid the smoke and confusion of battle, Willard ordered his men forward into the tangled growth of the Plum Valley swale. Some of the men were shouting, "Remember Harpers Ferry!" as they advanced, bayonets lowered, and "hurled themselves upon the advancing foe." Under this final onslaught, Barksdale's exhausted men began to falter. The general, still on horseback, was "almost frantic with rage" as he watched his men start to retreat, but then he was struck several times and fell to the ground with mortal wounds. Willard was also killed during the fight.[28]

Throughout the afternoon and evening, Meade and Hancock had been forced to take men out of their line and hurl them into the fighting, piecemeal, as the fighting unrolled north across the fields, woods, and hills south of town. As a result, gaps opened in the Union position. McGilvery managed to patch one of those with his artillery. The 1st Minnesota plugged another.

The regiment, commanded by Col. William Colvill, was waiting on Cemetery Ridge near the gap left by Caldwell. Approaching from the west were Alabamians of Cadmus Wilcox's brigade. Hancock—who appeared to be everywhere on the field this day—rode up, aghast to see that only the 1st Minnesota stood between Wilcox and Cemetery Ridge. "My God! Are these all the men we have here?" he asked. He pointed toward the enemy. "Advance, Colonel, and take those colors," he ordered. Colville and his regiment made a desperate charge, suffering 68 percent casualties during the struggle. But they managed to slow the Confederates long enough for Union reinforcements to arrive.

Further to the north, Gen. Ambrose Wright claimed that he and his brigade of Georgians from Richard Anderson's II Corps division actually reached the top of Cemetery Ridge. "We were now complete masters of the field, having gained the key, as it were, of the enemy's whole line," Wright wrote, and he said he would have held it, had he been supported. (One enduring mystery is why brigade commander William Mahone of Anderson's division refused to send any of his men to help.) Not everyone was convinced that Wright made it that far. "Wright's story of the battle should be included among the better Civil War romances," said noted Gettysburg historian Edward Coddington. Abner

Doubleday of the I Corps, however, believed that Wright's claim was true. "On this occasion Wright did what Lee failed to accomplish the next day at such a heavy expense of life, *for he pierced our centre*, and held it for a short time," wrote Doubleday.[29]

Wright's men came close enough, at least for George Gordon Meade. The army commander rode up to Cemetery Ridge late in the day and found no Union soldiers between him and the oncoming Georgians. "He straightens himself in his stirrups, as do also the aides who now ride closer to him, bracing themselves up to meet the crisis," recalled Meade's son, who served as one of his aides. "It is in the minds of those who follow him that he is going to throw himself into the breach—anything to gain a few moments' time." The general drew his sword. Then reinforcements arrived from the I Corps (now commanded by John Newton, whom Meade trusted more than he trusted Doubleday). Yet another crisis had passed. When Newton reached Meade, the two generals shared Newton's flask and were showered by dirt from an exploding shell. Someone remarked that things had looked pretty desperate. "Yes," Meade replied, "but it is all right now."

But the fighting was not quite over. Late on July 2, as darkness descended on a brutal and bloody day, two brigades of Jubal Early's division tried to do what Richard Ewell had earlier decided was not "practicable"—to take Cemetery Hill. The attack began at dusk. In the increasing gloom, Harry Hays's Louisiana brigade and Isaac Avery's North Carolinians moved quietly out of town and into the fields north of the hill, masked by the growing darkness and the rolling terrain. Once they spotted the enemy, Union artillery opened fire. "But on, still on, they came, moving steadily to the assault, soon the infantry opened fire, but they never faltered," said an Ohio soldier. "They moved forward as steadily, amid this hail of shot shell and Minnie ball, as though they were on parade far removed from danger."[30] Standing between the Rebels and success were the soldiers of Francis Barlow's XI Corps division, now under the command of Adelbert Ames. They fell back under the unexpected onslaught. The Rebels continued into the Union artillery positions on East Cemetery Hill. At points the fighting was hand-to-hand, with the artillerymen clubbing their adversaries with sponge staffs and rammers. Alerted by the tumult, Hancock dispatched the II Corps Brigade of Samuel Carroll. Without support, the Rebels had no choice but to retreat.

Dan Sickles's decision to move his III Corps forward on July 2 had reverberations all along the Union line. That afternoon, desperate to support the beleaguered III Corps, Meade ordered the XII Corps' Henry Slocum to send reinforcements from Culp's Hill, on the far right of the Union fishhook. The only men left behind to defend the position belonged to George Greene's brigade. At sixty-two, Greene was the oldest Union general on the field. He was a Rhode Islander and a West Point graduate who had been working as an engineer when the war broke out. He used his engineering skills to great effect at Culp's Hill, overseeing his brigade's construction of entrenchments.

Greene's fortifications proved their worth when the Rebels of Maj. Gen. Edward Johnson's II Corps division began making their way up the wooded slope in the gathering darkness. The Rebels didn't have a chance when the first volley hit them. "The light from the muzzle blasts of hundreds of Greene's muskets lit the woods like day, revealing Johnson's confederates massed below," remembered one soldier.[31] During the night, Greene's men fought off attack after attack. "They acted bravely, they came as close as they could but very few got within 2 rods of us, those that did never went away again," wrote one soldier from the 149th New York.[32] The woods of Culp's Hill were soon covered with the dead and dying.

However, Greene was not able to defend the entire XII Corps position, even with help from I Corps and II Corps reinforcements, and soldiers from George Steuart's brigade captured a portion of the works on the right of the line. When the tired and footsore XII Corps soldiers returned to Culp's Hill from the Union left, they found their old positions occupied by Rebels, leading to some confusion and mistaken identity in the darkness. The fighting petered out sometime around ten o'clock, and the two sides hunkered down and waited to resume the struggle in the morning.

On the night of July 2, George Meade called his generals together for a meeting at his headquarters, a tiny white farmhouse on the east slope of Cemetery Ridge. Dan Sickles was not there. A cannonball had struck him in the leg during the fight that afternoon, and a doctor had amputated the smashed limb and sent Sickles on his way to Washington, D.C. There he started a lifelong campaign to justify his actions and denigrate Meade. According to Sickles's version of events, by moving his corps forward and precipitating the fighting on July 2, he prevented Meade from retreating. "General Sickles apparently preferred to be guilty of wilful insubordination than of stupidity," wrote historian Coddington.[33]

Meade and his generals met in the back room of the two-room house. Warren, slightly wounded in the neck on Little Round Top, lay down on the bed and promptly fell asleep. The other generals discussed the day's events and the army's condition until Daniel Butterfield, Meade's chief of staff, suggested they vote on the strategy for the morning. The feeling was unanimous that the Army of the Potomac should remain in its present position and wait for Lee to attack. "Such then is the decision," Meade said, and the generals diverged to their respective commands. Before John Gibbon rode off, Meade talked to him. "If Lee attacks tomorrow, it will be on *your front*," Meade said. The Rebels had tried attacking the left and the right. Meade figured they would make an attempt on the center next.[34]

It had been a day of brutal combat all along the Union line, from the 20th Maine at the far left on Little Round Top to the 137th New York on the far right on Culp's Hill. At no point had the "fishhook" been breached for any length of time. Still, Lee felt confident about ultimate success. "The result of this day's operations induced the belief that, with proper concert of action, and with the increased support that the positions gained on the right would enable the artillery to render the assaulting columns, we should ultimately succeed, and it was accordingly determined to continue the attack," Lee later reported to Confederate president Jefferson Davis.

July 3, 1863

THE FIGHTING FOR CULP'S HILL ERUPTED EARLY, WITH NORTHERNERS AND Southerners launching their attacks around dawn. The Federals began their effort with a cannonade to wreak havoc among the Southern soldiers in their captured entrenchments. One Rebel officer said "the whole hillside seemed enveloped in a blaze."[35] Then it was up to the infantries, as men from Pennsylvania, New York, Ohio, Maryland (on both sides), Louisiana, Alabama, North Carolina, and Virginia carried out a furious battle for the rugged terrain of Culp's Hill. The Union soldiers had the upper hand, especially Greene's brigade, which had the dual advantages of their breastworks and a commanding position above boulder-strewn and steep approaches.

The story of the 149th New York's flag testifies to the intensity of the firefight. Bullets knocked the flag down twice, pierced it eighty times, and shattered the staff a couple of times. Sgt. William C. Lilly managed to splice the staff back together both times, a scene depicted in a bas relief on the regiment's monument. The number of dead and wounded Confederate soldiers strewn on the ground in front of Greene's defenses provided even more sobering evidence of the struggle's ferocity. When the fighting ended around eleven o'clock that morning, the Union forces retained control of Culp's Hill. "The enemy were too securely entrenched and in too great numbers to be dislodged by the force at my command," Edward Johnson reported.[36]

Robert E. Lee had attacked the Union left and its right. Now he was determined to make an attack on the center. On the morning of July 3, Longstreet once again tried to persuade Lee to move around the Union left, and once again Lee refused. He pointed at Cemetery Hill. "The enemy is there, and I am going to strike him," said Lee.

Longstreet said later that he told Lee such an attack was doomed to fail, that the Union position was too strong. Lee, he said, seemed "impatient" by Longstreet's continued intransigence. But orders were orders. Longstreet, despite being despondent over what he saw as a doomed attempt that would send hundreds if not thousands of men to their deaths, had no choice but to take charge of the attack. "With my knowledge of the situation, I could see the desperate and hopeless nature of the charge and the cruel slaughter it would cause," he said.[37]

Some historians insist that Pickett's Charge should be called "Longstreet's Assault," or perhaps the "Pickett-Pettigrew-Trimble Assault," because George Pickett commanded only one of the three divisions involved. After the war, North Carolinians would be particularly incensed at the way Virginia's role in the attack overshadowed the soldiers from the Tar Heel State who had also fought and died.

Pickett was a Southern cavalier with perfumed ringlets of hair. His division was fresh, having reached the field the day before without seeing action. James Pettigrew was in command of Henry Heth's division, Heth having been wounded during the first day's fighting. After Dorsey Pender had been mortally wounded on July 2, James Lane had taken command of his division, but less than an hour before the attack commenced Lee replaced Lane with Isaac Trimble. A general without portfolio, Trimble had been traveling with Richard Ewell, who had grown tired of Trimble's unsolicited advice. Lane returned to his brigade.

Of the three divisions involved in the initial attack, only one came from Longstreet's corps. Still, Lee gave his "old war horse" responsibility for the attack, despite Longstreet's strongly voiced reservations. Like his actions on July 2, Longstreet's conduct of the fight on July 3 would receive harsh criticism after the war.

Lee planned to open his assault with a devastating artillery barrage and then attack with three divisions of infantry, accompanied by strong artillery support. The attack started around one o'clock that hot afternoon, when two guns of the Washington Artillery each fired a single shot. Then all hell seemed to break loose as some 160 Rebel cannon opened up on the Federal lines. The Union guns, about 130 of them, replied in kind. The result was a man-made thunder supposedly heard as far away as Pittsburgh. "We were not unfamiliar with artillery fire but this proved to be something far beyond all previous experience, or conception, and the scene was terrific beyond description," remembered one Union soldier. Charles Wainwright, who commanded the artillery in the I Corps, said, "For two hours the roar was continuous and loud as that from the falls of Niagara."[38]

"I have read many accounts of this artillery duel, but the most graphic description by the most able writers falls far short of the reality," wrote an officer from the Irish Brigade. "No tongue or pen can find language strong enough to convey any idea of its awfulness. Streams of screaming projectiles poured through the hot air, falling and bursting everywhere. Men and horses were torn limb from limb; caissons exploded one after another in rapid succession, blowing the gunners to pieces. No spot within our lines was free from this frightful iron rain."[39]

The Confederates also suffered under the barrage. "The very atmosphere seemed broken by the rush and crash of projectiles, solid shot, shrieking, bursting shells," wrote a sergeant with the 9th Virginia who recalled seeing "guns, swords, haversacks, human flesh and bone, flying and dangling in the air, or bouncing above the earth as if shaken by an earthquake."[40]

Spectacular it may have been, but the Confederate artillery was not especially effective. The Rebels were plagued by poor ammunition. Many of their shells flew over the Union line and exploded on the far side of Cemetery Ridge—certainly bad for the men in the rear (and for General Meade's headquarters), but not so much for the men on the front lines. "Viewed as a display of fireworks, the Rebel practice was entirely successful, but as a military demonstration it was the biggest humbug of the season," said one Massachusetts artilleryman. Henry Hunt had his Union guns stop firing, hoping to lull the enemy into a false impression of their cannons' effectiveness. Hancock, however, insisted his guns remain active as a way to bolster his soldiers' morale. (This war of wills between the two Union generals led to years of postwar bickering and recrimination.[41])

Accounts about how long the cannonade lasted range from ninety minutes to two hours. Finally, the terrible cacophony died into silence. A private in the 69th Pennsylvania no doubt echoed the thoughts of many soldiers when he recalled that the advance of the Confederate infantry came as a relief after the terrible cannonade. "No holiday display seemed more imposing, nor troops on parade more regular, than this division of Pickett's Rebels," he wrote. "They came steadily arms at a trail, their appearance was truly a relief from that terrible fire of their artillery; not that it was so destructive, but the dread it occasioned, the range seemed so low, and the air so thick with flying missiles, that we did not enjoy any space of relief from the dread of being ploughed into shreds, until the appearance of the infantry when the fire slackened."[42]

Pickett's three brigades formed on the left. Pettigrew and his four brigades were on the right. Trimble's division, with two brigades, followed. Should this initial attack meet with success, Pickett could call on the III Corps brigades of Lang and Wilcox. All told, there were some 12,000 men in the initial attack, with another 5,000 available in reserve.

The Rebels had up to 1,450 yards of undulating farmland to cross on their way to Cemetery Ridge. Along the way they had to deal with rail fences that broke up their lines and an increasing storm of artillery shot and shell as they attempted to maintain their formations. Men fell by the score, but the survivors reformed their lines and kept marching. "Forward, still forward," wrote an officer of the 19th Virginia. "How thin the ranks are getting."[43]

James Lewis Armistead commanded a brigade in Pickett's division. "He kept fifteen or twenty steps in front of his brigade all the way, was cheering all the time calling his men to follow," said a lieutenant in the 53rd Virginia.[44] At some point Armistead placed his black hat atop his sword and held it high so his men could spot him in the smoke and confusion.

As the Rebels marched across the fields, Pickett's division made an oblique turn to the left in order to maintain contact with Pettigrew's division, or perhaps to correct its course toward a prominent grove of trees on the ridge ahead. By so doing, the Virginians provided a green brigade of Vermont troops a prime opportunity to pour a murderous fire into their flank.

The Vermont Brigade, five regiments of nine-month men under Brig. Gen. George Stannard, had been experiencing an uneventful time in the Washington defenses until it was suddenly called forth on June 23 and told to report to General Reynolds of the I Corps. The green troops embarked on a grueling series of marches to catch up with the Army of the Potomac. Now, on the afternoon of July 3, Stannard saw that from their position on the ridge, his men were perfectly placed to move forward, pivot to the right, and fire into Pickett's flank. The fire was devastating. On the opposite side of the Rebel force, the 8th Ohio found itself in a similar position and poured a deadly fire into John Brockenbrough's brigade of Pettigrew's division, eventually causing it to halt and retreat.

The fire on the flanks was bad enough. Along Cemetery Ridge, many Union soldiers had picked up abandoned weapons and loaded them, giving them multiple guns ready for the assault. They began to pour a deadly rain of fire into the oncoming Rebels. "The men fell like stalks of grain before the reaper but still they closed the gaps and pressed forward through that pitiless storm," said an officer in the 53rd Virginia.[45]

Alexander Webb commanded the Philadelphia Brigade, four Pennsylvania regiments that were positioned on Cemetery Ridge and now became the focus of the advancing Rebels. The 69th Pennsylvania was behind a low stone fence that ran north to south then turned at an abrupt angle to the east before resuming its north-south direction. This bend would gain renown as the "Bloody Angle." Webb, only twenty-eight, was new to brigade command, having been promoted on June 23.

Armistead led a small band of survivors through the hail of bullets and over the stone wall. "Boys, give them the cold steel!" he shouted.

"When they were over the fence the Army of the Potomac was nearer being whipped than it was at any time of the battle," Webb wrote to his wife on July 6. Armistead got far enough to place his hands on a Union cannon before being shot down with mortal wounds. "Men fall in heaps, still fighting, bleeding, dying," remembered one Confederate.[46]

That small foothold by Armistead and his men was not enough. Union reinforcements poured into the breech. "On the way to the wall we were advancing and firing and they were advancing and firing, this was kept up until we came hand-to-hand in some instances," remembered a soldier from the 72nd Pennsylvania of Webb's brigade, which had been waiting on the crest of the ridge in the rear. "We had quite a little dispute before we came to the stone wall; we fought hand to hand and clubbed guns, any way at all; each man picked out his man, that lasted a very short time and they fell back, what was left of them." (The 72nd Pennsylvania became the subject of bitter controversy after the war over the placement of its monument at the Angle. Other units said the 72nd had not gone that far forward until the fighting was over, and the dispute over the monument's location went all the way to the Pennsylvania Supreme Court before being decided in the regiment's favor.[47])

The Rebels who made it to Cemetery Ridge either fell dead, were wounded, were captured, or began to retreat. Longstreet, convinced that the charge had failed, refused to send in more troops. That decision, plus his slowness on July 2 and his willingness to criticize Lee after the war, helped make Longstreet a scapegoat for the loss at Gettysburg and drew the ire of many Confederate veterans.

Somewhere around 5,000 Confederates became casualties of the attack, either dead, wounded, or taken prisoner. Lee met some of the defeated survivors back on Seminary Ridge. "It is all my fault," he told them. When Lee found Pickett, devastated by the repulse of his men, Lee told him to ready his division to stop an enemy counterattack. "General Lee, I have no division now," Pickett replied.[48]

In the years since, veterans and historians have debated the attack's probability of success. "The arguments will no doubt continue for as long as people maintain an interest in the greatest battle ever fought on American soil," wrote military historian Mark Adkin.[49]

J EB STUART PLAYED NO ROLE IN THE FIGHTING AT GETTYSBURG UNTIL THE last day of the battle. With about 3,000 cavalrymen, Stuart swept around the Union right and prepared to attack the Federals from behind. Instead, he came up against some 3,250 Union cavalrymen commanded by Brig. Gen. David M. Gregg. Joining Gregg was a brigade under George Armstrong Custer, newly promoted to brigadier general. Custer's brigade belonged to Judson Kilpatrick's division, but Gregg had asked him to stay. Eager for a fight, Custer agreed.

The clash between the rival cavalries began with a spirited artillery duel before Stuart's men advanced on horseback from their shelter in the woods near the Rummel farm. These were the brigades of Brig. Gens. Wade Hampton and Fitzhugh Lee. "A grander spectacle than their advance has rarely been beheld," wrote a member of the 3rd Pennsylvania Cavalry. "They marched with well-aligned fronts and steady reins. Their polished saber-blades dazzled in the sun." Custer, just as thirsty for glory as Stuart was, shouted, "Come on, you wolverines!" and led a charge of his men. The rival cavalries crashed together, using sabers and pistols and filling the air with oaths and orders. Eventually the Rebels gave way, and Stuart's attempt was blunted.

Meanwhile, Kilpatrick, on the opposite end of the line south of the Round Tops, attempted his own cavalry charge. An impetuous, ambitious soldier, Kilpatrick had been recently promoted to general. Hoping to make an impact of his own, on the afternoon of July 3 "Kill-cavalry" ordered brigade commander Elon Farnsworth to charge the enemy on his front. According to some accounts, when Farnsworth protested that the terrain was ill-suited for a cavalry attack, Kilpatrick accused him of cowardice. (According to other accounts, this never happened.) But the rocky terrain did prove to be a poor place for a cavalry charge, and Farnsworth and his men found themselves boxed in by soldiers of Law's brigade, some of the same men who had tried to conquer Little Round Top the day before. Farnsworth was killed trying to fight his way back to his own lines. His death provided a sad coda to the fighting on July 3.

Should Meade have ordered an immediate counterattack after the repulse of Pickett's Charge? Hancock, badly wounded at the climax of the fight on July 3, thought so, and while lying on the battlefield he penned a note to Meade expressing that view. Meade examined the situation and even threw some skirmishers forward on the left, but decided that by the time he got his battered army into condition for an attack, it would have been too late in the day. Armchair generals have debated his decision ever since.

Even more have argued about Meade's pursuit of Lee after the Army of Northern Virginia pulled out of Gettysburg on July 5. Meade did mount a pursuit and appeared to have the Rebel army bottled up against the Potomac River in Williamsport, Maryland, with the river too high to ford and the pontoon bridge the Confederates had used to cross from Virginia destroyed. On the night of July 12, Meade held another consultation with his generals. All but two—Alfred Pleasonton and Otis Howard, still seeking that redemption he had been seeking since Chancellorsville—advised reconnoitering the enemy defenses before attacking. Meade decided to wait another day. When he moved his army forward on July 14, he found that Lee's army had disappeared across the Potomac. Among the most disappointed by the news was President Abraham Lincoln. "I do not believe you appreciate the magnitude of the misfortune involved in Lee's escape," Lincoln wrote in a letter to Meade that he ultimately did not send. "He was within your easy grasp, and to have closed upon him would, in connection with our other late successes, have ended the war. As it is, the war will be prolonged indefinitely."[50]

Was Lincoln right? Could Meade have captured Lee's army and ended the war? As might be expected, debate on that issue continues to this day.

The Army of Northern Virginia brought about 72,000 men to Gettysburg. When the fighting ended, 4,708 of those soldiers had been killed, 12,693 had been wounded, and another 5,830 were missing or captured. Of the Army of the Potomac's 95,000 men, 3,155 were dead, 14,530 had been wounded, and 5,369 were missing or captured. The three-day battle was the bloodiest of the Civil War. The land around Gettysburg was a charnel house. Dead soldiers were buried where they lay. Piles of dead horses were set on fire. In town, public buildings, and many private ones, were pressed into service as hospitals. Some Gettysburg citizens dealt with the stink of death and decay by carrying bottles of peppermint oil to dab under their noses. Amazingly, only one citizen had been killed during the fighting. Virginia "Jennie" Wade had been baking bread at her sister's house just south of Cemetery Hill when a bullet tore through a door and into her back, killing her instantly. Today she lies in a grave in Evergreen Cemetery.

More than a century and a half after the end of the American Civil War, Gettysburg exerts a pull on the imagination. Each year sees more books published about the conflict, many of them casting old controversies in new light, not always successfully. Millions of tourists visit the military park each year to take a tour or walk in the footsteps of those men who fought so many years ago.

One of those men was Joshua Lawrence Chamberlain, who earned his place in history on the southern slope of Little Round Top. Chamberlain returned to Gettysburg in October 1889 to participate in the dedication of monuments to his fellow Maine soldiers. On October 3 he made a speech that is still quoted today. It captures the allure of this great battlefield—the place where so many men, Northern and Southern, gave "their last full measure of devotion."

"In great deeds something abides," Chamberlain said. "On great fields something stays. Forms change and pass; bodies disappear; but spirits linger, to consecrate ground for the vision-place of souls. And reverent men and women from afar, and generations that know us not and that we know not of, heart-drawn to see where and by whom great things were suffered and done for them, shall come to this deathless field, to ponder and dream; and lo! the shadow of a mighty presence shall wrap them in its bosom, and the power of the vision pass into their souls."

One thing is certain—the battle of Gettysburg will continue to stimulate the imagination, inspire debate, and provoke discussion for years to come.

Notes

1. J. David Petruzzi, "Battle of Gettysburg: Who Really Fired the First Shot," *America's Civil War*, July 2006, http://www.historynet.com/battle-of-gettysburg-who-really-fired-the-first-shot.htm. For 9th New York, see *Battles and Leaders* III, 275.
2. Porter, 222.
3. Calef from OR, Vol. 27, pt. 1, p. 1031.
4. Coddington, 682 note 14.
5. Coddington, 686, note 46.
6. OR, Vol. 27, pt 1, 245.
7. Quoted in *Maine Roads to Gettysburg*.
8. Dawes, 169.
9. Gottfried, 539.
10. Hartwig, "11th Army Corps" in the *Gettysburg Magazine* no. 2.
11. Barlow, "Fear Was Not in Him," 161.
12. Gallagher, *The First Day at Gettysburg*, 55.
13. *Battles and Leaders*, III, 302.
14. Quotes from *Battles and Leaders* III, 246 and 339.
15. Smith, A Famous Batter, 103.
16. Quote from Smith, 138.
17. Oates, 219.
18. Quoted in *Through Blood and Fire*, 85.
19. Dedication of the 20th Maine Monuments.
20. Quoted in Daniel M. Laney, "Wasted Gallantry: Hood's Texas Brigade at Gettysburg," *Gettysburg Magazine*, no. 16 (1997): 27–45.
21. Quoted in Brian A. Bennett, "The Supreme Event in Its Existence: The 140th New York on Little Round Top," *Gettysburg Magazine*, no. 3 (1990): 17–25.
22. Quoted in Garry E. Adelman, "Hazlett's Battery at Gettysburg," *Gettysburg Magazine*, no. 21 (1999).
23. Gottfried, 119.
24. Barett, "Old Fourth Michigan," 22; Quote from Bachelder, p. 1071.
25. OR, 612.
26. OR, Vol. 27, Pt. 1, 653–54.
27. OR, p. 882.
28. See Campbell, "Willard's Brigade," *Gettysburg Magazine*, no. 7.
29. For quotes, see Gottfried, "Wright's Charge," *Gettysburg Magazine*, no. 17; Coddington, 422; Doubleday, 176.
30. Bachelder, 745.
31. Gottfried, 148; Cox, 118–19.
32. Gottfried, 390.
33. Coddington, 347.
34. Gibbon, 145.
35. Pfanz, Culp's Hill, 291.
36. Quoted in Adkin, 461.
37. Annals of the War, 429; *Battles and Leaders* III, 343.
38. Quotes from Hess, 127, and Nevins (Wainwright), 248.
39. Mulholland, 412.
40. Quoted in Rollins, 98.
41. Quote in Rollins, *Pickett's Charge!*, 124.
42. Bachelder papers, 1406-on.
43. Rollins, 181.
44. Rollins, 183.
45. Quoted in Rollins, 163.
46. Rollins, 180.
47. Testimony in the Adams County Court of Common Pleas, about the 72nd PA Monument case. See my notes for the 72nd PA article, pages 136-on.
48. See Rollins, 143.
49. Adkin, 496.
50. See "Lincoln's Unsent Letter to George Meade" (July 14, 1863), American Battlefield Trust, https://www.battlefields.org/learn/primary-sources/lincolns-unsent-letter-george-meade.

Brandy Station Review

June 8, 1863

QUICKLY ROLLING UP HIS BEDROLL IN THE DARKNESS BEHIND THE
Rappahannock River near Fredericksburg, a Confederate surgeon
penned a hurried note to his wife, a short missive containing momentous news: "The Army is moving," he gravely wrote. Thrusting the scrawled
message to a courier, the physician swung up onto a wagon that followed a
fast-moving infantry file. Soon the gray ranks resolutely disappeared into the
night, headed toward the center of Virginia's great Piedmont, Culpeper County.

And so it came to pass on June 3, 1863, that America's threshold military event, the Pennsylvania campaign, was secretly set in motion, and Robert E. Lee's Army of Northern Virginia stole a march on the Army of the Potomac, concentrated just across the river at Falmouth. After soundly defeating but not destroying Maj. Gen. Joe Hooker's command less than a month earlier at Chancellorsville, General Lee seized the strategic initiative from his still-demoralized opponent and boldly transferred the "scene of hostilities" northward from Virginia.

Numerous objectives—logistical, political, and military—underpinned Robert E. Lee's decision to invade the North, but his abiding purpose for facing Pennsylvania was a resolve to obliterate "those people" once and for all. Like the fierce Hannibal, Lee "genuinely wanted to fight," but unlike the battle-obsessed Cathaginian, Lee desired to fight one last time. And he wanted to win.

Crossing the Rapidan at Raccoon Ford into Culpeper County alongside his wading foot soldiers on June 7, the gray man on the gray horse gazed into the faces of saluting cavalry videttes. Ordered beyond the army's left into Culpeper by Lee shortly after Chancellorsville, Maj. Gen. James E. B. Stuart's Cavalry Division had been picketing the upper crossings of the Rappahannock while concentrating and foraging the five brigades and 10,000 troopers of Lee's mounted arm.

General Lee proceeded with his staff into Culpeper Court House and paid his compliments to Eastern View's matriarch, Mrs. Sarah Freeman. After Lee's aides erected his shelter in Eastern View's yard, the army chief retired to his tent and wrote a brief "request" to his cavalry chieftain. Soon thereafter, an out-of-breath messenger appeared at Jeb Stuart's Fleetwood Hill headquarters fronting the Rappahannock, near Brandy Station. Almost immediately, Stuart's couriers galloped out in all directions toward his far-flung brigade commanders, ferrying each an important order: "Prepare your brigade for review tomorrow by Commanding General R. E. Lee."

Jeb Stuart earlier invited General Lee to review the cavalry division (on June 5), but Lee conducted this very public review for far different motives than the mere indulgence of his young cavalry commander. Ironically, however, General Lee's purpose in mandating a review was based on an invalid assumption by Lee himself that General Hooker had already discovered that the bulk of the Southern army had left Fredericksburg. It is clear that Joe Hooker had absolutely no idea on June 7 that Lee was in Culpeper County with two full corps of his army (Ewell's and Longstreet's). Falsely surmising that his movement to Culpeper had been discovered by the enemy (as his post-Gettysburg report states), the last thing Lee wanted was for his enemy to retrograde back into the impregnable defenses of Washington. Highlighting this concern, Lee wrote on June 8 of his desire to draw the Union Army "out in a position to be assailed." To be sure, Lee now wanted his enemy to know that he was on the move. "Here I am," Lee says as this scenario plays out. "Catch me if you can, Joe Hooker."

Mounted on his famous warhorse, Traveller, and accompanied by artillery chief William N. Pendleton, General Lee trotted out from Eastern View about midday on June 8, soon arriving at the review grounds about the railhead of

Inlet Station. Gathered on the treeless, open plain beneath the review knoll, Jeb Stuart's Cavalry Division, the finest light cavalry on the face of the earth, awaited. "Getting right down to business at a full run" and escorted by General Stuart and his staff, along with Pendleton, Lee galloped down the front of the mile-long first line (there were three such files). "Erupting from the earth," General Lee immediately received the spontaneous "salute of thousands of upraised sabers." As Lee's cortege continued to "thunder along," an observant trooper observed that the army commander "seemed in buoyant spirits . . . and his easy posture and soldierlike mien . . . made the blood tingle through the veins in every cavalryman." Focused on his personal inspection, General Lee didn't notice that several members of his entourage couldn't keep up as they "succumbed to ditches . . . with their hats gone off, and led their mounts most dejectedly away."

The long review finally over and called a "splendid success," a participant later wrote: "Many a young man rode proudly past the commanding general that day, who, before another day's sun had sunk . . . fought his last battle." But no one knew that then, and General Lee returned to the Court House. Heading toward the river, Jeb Stuart retired his division at a slow walk back to their camps situated in concentric circles around Brandy Station. On the late afternoon of June 8, Lee prepared his army to move across the Rappahannock toward the Blue Ridge on the early morning of June 9. But during the night of June 8, other forces—these wearing blue—moved stealthily down to the Rappahannock. Hunting out their counterparts for the first time in the war, the Cavalry Corps of the Army of the Potomac had come to kill the king. On the morning of June 9, 1863, the Northerners crossed the river first. In so doing, the blue horse inaugurated both the Gettysburg campaign and the largest cavalry battle of the war—both events of no small distinction in American history.

CLARK B. HALL is a historian and preservationist who has written widely on the role of cavalry in the American Civil War. In 2012 he received the Civil War Trust's Lifetime Achievement Award in recognition of his twenty-five-year efforts to protect America's hallowed ground.

The Battle of Brandy Station

THE UNION CAVALRY HAD LITTLE TO SHOW FOR ITSELF DURING THE FIRST two years of the war. "Who ever saw a dead cavalryman?" was a jibe directed at the mounted soldiers. The battle of Brandy Station changed that on June 9, 1863. It was the largest cavalry battle ever fought in North America, pitting 11,000 Union forces (including some infantry) against 9,500 Confederates. It was not a Union victory—the Federals ceded ground to their Confederate adversaries—but it demonstrated that the blue-clad horsemen were finally a force to be reckoned with.

Maj. Gen. Alfred Pleasonton had recently replaced George Stoneman as head of the Army of the Potomac's cavalry corps. When army commander Joseph Hooker received intelligence that the Confederate cavalry under James Ewell Brown "Jeb" Stuart was assembling near Brandy Station, Virginia, on Orange & Alexandria Railroad, apparently to prepare for a raid, Hooker ordered Pleasonton to surprise the Rebels.

Neither Hooker nor Pleasonton realized that the Rebel gathering was actually a precursor to Robert E. Lee's planned push north into Pennsylvania. Before embarking on the campaign, though, Stuart indulged his love of pageantry by holding a grand review of his men—two reviews, actually, because Lee had been unable to attend the first one.

Pleasonton unwittingly took advantage of Stuart's inattention to launch his attack. Cavalrymen in John Buford's division, supported by two brigades of infantry, opened up the proceedings after crossing the Rappahannock River at Beverly Ford, surprising the Rebels there and pushing them back toward Fleetwood Hill, a prominent rise near the railroad where Stuart had his headquarters. Stuart was surprised, but he managed to rally and counterattack. At one point the contending cavalries became "a mingled mass, fighting and struggling with pistol and saber like maddened savages," as one Confederate recalled. Even supported by infantry, Buford's attack stalled.

Stuart was surprised again when he received word of a second attack on Fleetwood Hill, this one coming from the south. It was David McMurtrie Gregg's cavalry division, which had crossed the river at Kelly's Ford early that morning and found Fleetwood Hill undefended except for one howitzer. Stuart's aide, Maj. Henry B. McClellan, had the gun hastily rolled into position to confront the Union cavalry and sent messengers to Stuart for help. Stuart dispatched units to deal with this new threat and galloped back with them. They reached Fleetwood Hill just in time to blunt Gregg's initial attack.

One of Gregg's brigades was commanded by Judson Kilpatrick, a man whose willingness to sacrifice his men and horses earned him the nickname of "Kill-Cavalry." Stuart's men threw back Kilpatrick's initial attack in some disorder. Kilpatrick, frustrated, rode up to Calvin Douty, commander of the 1st Maine Cavalry. "Colonel, what can you do with your regiment?" Kilpatrick demanded.

"I can drive the rebels to hell," Douty replied. One Maine horseman described the resulting fight as "a grand, moving panorama of war." Sabers slashed, pistols fired, horses whinnied, dust flew, and men died. "It was a scene to be witnessed but once in a lifetime, and one well worth the risks of battle to witness," said the Maine man. The first charge pushed the Rebels off the hill, but the Confederates regrouped, charged again, and forced the Union soldiers back.

"Fresh columns of the enemy arriving upon the ground received the vigorous charges of my regiments, and, under the heavy blows of our sabers, were in every instance driven back," Gregg reported. "Thus for an hour and a half was the contest continued, not in skirmishing, but in determined charges." Finally, lacking support, Gregg determined to fall back.

Sometime around five o'clock that afternoon, after a long, hard day of fighting, Pleasonton decided he had done enough and ordered a withdrawal. His forces made it back across the Rappahannock without difficulty.

It had been a near miss for Stuart and his cavalry, but they held the field. Still, the Federal horsemen had reason to feel satisfied. They had surprised Stuart, and they had fought well. "The cavalry fight at Brandy Station can hardly be called a *victory*," wrote one disgruntled Confederate. "Stuart was certainly surprised and but for the supreme gallantry of his subordinate officers and the men in his command it would have been a day of disaster and disgrace." Major McClellan, whose quick thinking on Fleetwood Hill helped stave off disaster for the Confederates, later noted "one result of incalculable importance" from the battle of Brandy Station: "It *made* the Federal cavalry."

TOM HUNTINGTON is the author of *Maine Roads to Gettysburg, Searching for George Gordon Meade: The Forgotten Victor of Gettysburg, Guide to Gettysburg Battlefield Monuments*, and *Pennsylvania Civil War Trails*. He lives in Camp Hill, Pennsylvania, about forty minutes from the Gettysburg battlefield.

The Gray Comanches

BRANDY STATION, VIRGINIA, APPROACHING NOON, JUNE 9, 1863. A VETERAN
Union cavalry division of 2,400 men under the command of Brig. Gen.
David McMurtrie Gregg had quietly arrived just east of the small village,
and the Yankees gazed covetously on a ridge hovering a half mile to their front.
The low-slung eminence, called Fleetwood Hill by locals, dominates the flat
landscape for miles around. It was the headquarters of Gen. J. E. B. Stuart, but he
was not there, and the Federals desired possession. From Brandy Station, Colonel

Percy Wyndham leads his brigade, consisting of the 1st New Jersey, 1st Pennsylvania, and 1st Maryland Cavalry Regiments, toward the hill, bringing up behind three guns of the 6th Battery, New York Light Artillery, Captain Joseph W. Martin commanding.

A mile and a half north of Fleetwood Hill, General Stuart was directing the resolute Confederate defense at St. James Church against Brig. Gen. John Buford's gallant assault thrusting down from Beverly Ford on the Rappahannock River. Hearing the shocking alarm that Yankees had arrived at his rear and were approaching his headquarters on Fleetwood, Stuart reacted quickly. Leaving Brig. Gen. W. H. F. "Rooney" Lee's brigade in place to oppose Buford, Stuart successively withdrew the vaunted cavalry brigades of Brig. Gens. William E. "Grumble" Jones and Wade Hampton from the St. James line and sent them thundering back to save Fleetwood and his headquarters.

Leading the gray horse over the wide meadow from St. James, the 12th Virginia galloped up Fleetwood and charged directly into the 1st New Jersey. Badly spread out, the 12th Virginia was summarily brushed away, and Fleetwood Hill was crowned with the blue cavalry. Closed up and spurring hard, the 35th Battalion Virginia Cavalry, the "Comanches," pounded directly for the ridge, screaming wildly, pistols and sabers high, Lt. Col. Elijah White leading.

Originally mustered into Confederate service as an independent command of partisans from Loudoun County, Virginia, the 35th Battalion was later joined by Maryland horsemen of Southern sympathy, as well as Virginians from Albemarle, Frederick, Page, and Shenandoah Counties. Against their free spirit preferences, the battalion was brought into regular service with "Grumble" Jones's Laurel Brigade. Fond of neither drill nor discipline, the fighters of the 35th were nevertheless of the first rank. Specializing in impetuous hit-and-run attacks, and accompanied by savage shrieks, they were dubbed the "Comanches." The 35th also had a habit, Wade Hampton said, of "riding over everything in sight," with "Old White" always in the fore. The "Comanches" embodied the spirit of their fiery commander "Lige" White.

Cap. Joseph Martin crossed Flat Run at the base of Fleetwood Hill and opened fire with canister at the Rebels on the ridge. The 6th New York Battery had distinguished itself a month earlier at Chancellorsville by standing tall amid the rout of the XI Corps, helping delay the onslaught of Stonewall Jackson's ferocious attack. The artillerists of the 6th New York were not disposed to flinch nor flee under fire, and they did not do so on this day.

Joined now by other Southern regiments on Fleetwood, the "Comanches" were reeling from Martin's withering cannon fire and a rolling flank assault from Col. Judson Kilpatrick's brigade storming up the southeastern slope of the ridge. Furious at the cannonading that "had been playing upon me the whole time," White ordered a fateful attack into the teeth of Martin's guns.

Down Fleetwood the "Comanches" flew to the flat, grassy plain beneath. "Through the terrible and destructive rain of grape and cannister and leaden bullets," the 35th raged into the spewing battery. "It became a hand-to-hand fight with pistol and sabre," Martin reported, and "never did men act with more coolness and bravery." White contended, "There was no demand for a surrender or offer of one until nearly all the men . . . were either killed or wounded." Captain Martin concluded, "Of the 36 men that I took into the engagement, but six came out safely . . . and scarcely one of them but will carry the honorable mark of the sabre or bullet to his grave."

Captain Martin's three guns would be lost, and "Lige" White would suffer his greatest losses of the war, nearly one hundred, during the battle, many at the hands of the 6th New York. After a steamrolling charge by Wade Hampton, Fleetwood Hill was cleared of Union cavalry, and the largest and most important cavalry battle of the Civil War, the battle of Brandy Station, was finally over.

CLARK B. HALL is a historian and preservationist who has written widely on the role of cavalry in the American Civil War. In 2012 he received the Civil War Trust's Lifetime Achievement Award in recognition of his twenty-five-year efforts to protect America's hallowed ground.

McPherson Ridge

July 1, 1863

AT ELEVEN IN THE MORNING ON JUNE 30, 1863, 2,900 WEARY FEDERAL cavalrymen rode into the town of Gettysburg. Organized in two brigades, these troopers were commanded by Brig. Gen. John Buford, their division commander. Buford was a thirty-six-year-old West Pointer who had seen many years of hard service in the West before the Civil War. Serving in the Second Dragoons, Buford had learned the value of mobility and of fighting dismounted. The quiet Kentuckian, modest and brave, was the consummate cavalry officer, unpretentious but competent and steady. Revered by his men, he was known as "Old Steadfast," a trait that served him well. He would need all of his talents at Gettysburg.

Arriving in the town, Buford, with a veteran's trained eye for terrain, recognized the strong defensive features of the ground in the area. Realizing that Culp's Hill, Cemetery Hill, Cemetery Ridge, and the Round Tops offered strong defensive positions, Buford chose McPherson Ridge for his main line of resistance and set about designing a defense in depth to the north and west of the town, where Confederate infantry was massing along the Chambersburg Pike.

Deploying the brigade of Col. William Gamble, of the 8th Illinois Cavalry, along either side of the Chambersburg Pike, and the brigade of Col. Thomas C. Devin, of the 6th New York Cavalry, to the north and east of the town, Buford also brought up Battery A, 2nd U.S. Artillery, commanded by Lt. John Calef, a fine young horse artillerist. Setting up vidette posts well to the west of McPherson Ridge, Buford established an effective early-warning system. That night, Buford held a council of war with Devin, Gamble, Calef, and his staff to discuss the next day's plans. Tom Devin, always spoiling for a fight, announced he would hold his position the next day. Buford, ever the realist, told Devin, "No, you won't. They will attack you in the morning and they will come booming—skirmishers three deep. You will have to fight like the devil to hold your own until supports arrive." As the meeting ended, Buford told his subordinates, "The enemy knows the importance of this position and will strain every nerve to secure it, and if we are able to hold it, we will do well." Buford's signal officer, A. Brainerd Jerome, noted that Buford "seemed anxious, more so than I ever saw him."

At about five o'clock in the morning on July 1, Lt. Marcellus E. Jones squeezed off a shot at the advancing Confederate infantry. Skirmish fire spread up and down the picket line as the surprised Confederates responded. Stopping to form a line of battle, nearly two hours passed before the Confederate infantry resumed its steady approach. Engaging Buford's troopers on Herr's Ridge, about a mile to the west of McPherson Ridge, the blue-clad horsemen held off the gray-clad infantry for nearly an hour. Finally forced back to McPherson Ridge by the sheer weight of the Confederate numbers, the Federal resistance stiffened.

Buford, accompanied only by his bugler, rode his lines atop his magnificent thoroughbred warhorse, Grey Eagle. Unafraid of the bullets and artillery shells falling around him, Buford calmly surveyed the field and made his dispositions. Meeting Calef as the young artillerist brought his guns to the field, Buford instructed him to deploy his three sections on a wide front to create the illusion he had more artillery support. Calef deployed one section on either side of the road near the McPherson barn, and another section about 800 yards away. His guns opened on the Confederates, and soon a fierce duel erupted between the batteries. Meanwhile, the Rebel advance continued, and it became a race for time—would Buford's beleaguered troopers be able to hold out until the Yankee infantry arrived on the scene?

At 9:30, just as the Federal horsemen were running out of ammunition, the Army of the Potomac's infantry arrived on the field and saved the day. Buford's men had performed admirably, buying time and stoutly defending the critical high ground surrounding the town that would become the main Union line of battle the next day. Later, John Buford proudly wrote, "The zeal, bravery, and good behavior of the officers and men on the night of June 30, and during July 1, was commendable in the extreme. A heavy task was before us; we were equal to it, and shall all remember with pride that at Gettysburg we did our country much service."

ERIC J. WITTENBERG has spent years studying the role of the Federal cavalry in the Gettysburg campaign and has written extensively on the role played by Gen. John Buford and his troopers. He is author or coauthor of numerous books about the Civil War, including *The Devil's to Pay: John Buford at Gettysburg* and *Protecting the Flank at Gettysburg: The Battles for Brinkerhoff's Ridge and East Cavalry Field, July 2–3, 1863.*

"For God's Sake Forward"

2nd Regiment Wisconsin Volunteers, Iron Brigade

O N THE MORNING OF JULY 1, 1863, AS THE 302 MEN AND OFFICERS OF the 2nd Wisconsin Infantry marched toward the small town of Gettysburg, they had no means of knowing what part they would play in shaping the battle to come. Dressed in the black hats that had become their trademark, they were proud of their brigade's new status as the 1st Brigade of the 1st Division of the I Corps of the Army of the Potomac. That pride had been hard-won. They had left Wisconsin in 1861 over 1,000 men strong. After experiencing First Bull Run, they joined what would later be known as the "Iron Brigade." Bloodied at Brawner's Farm, the 2nd withstood the attacks of Stonewall Jackson's men even when two out of every three men in the ranks had fallen. As the war progressed, their reputation grew, even as their ranks thinned.

Drawing near the town, they could hear firing in the distance. Some of the men, aware that a fight might be in the offing and worried that their rifles were rusty from the evening damp, snapped caps to clear them out. Normally this would bring a quick reprimand from their officers, but that day there was none, giving silent confirmation that the officers also felt the seriousness of the day. Soon aides of Gen. John F. Reynolds, their commander, led them off the road, and they hurried forward toward the sound of the fighting.

West of town, on McPherson Ridge, General Reynolds had delayed the enemy through Gen. John Buford's cavalry and the 2nd Brigade of Gen. James Wadsworth's 1st Division of I Corps. Then, through the smoke, Lt. Col. John A. Kress, one of Wadsworth's aides, pointed out a mass of men—the battle-hardened Confederate brigade of Gen. James Archer—moving toward the left of the Union line. Realizing this force would soon cross Willoughby Run into the woodlot to their left, thereby flanking Cutler's already engaged line, Kress was ordered to find the first unit he could to plug this important gap in the Federal line.

Kress spurred his horse back toward the Seminary on the ridge to their rear and, upon cresting it, encountered the Iron Brigade. At the head of the column was the 2nd Wisconsin, led by its colonel, Lucius Fairchild. There was no time to find the brigade's commander to coordinate the attack, so Kress ordered the colonel "to form his regiment forward into line," telling Fairchild "he would find the enemy to his front as soon as he could form." Surprised at this order, Fairchild replied that his men's rifles were unloaded, but Kress said that he could not wait. Not knowing what was before them but sensing the urgency of the moment, Fairchild called for the field and staff officers to dismount and the regiment to form into line. Moving to obey, the men heard the command to load on the run and fix bayonets. Ahead of them lay a grove of trees on McPherson Ridge.

Seeing the 2nd advancing, Reynolds rode to meet them and to lead them on. Drawing near, he called out, "Forward men, forward for God's sake and drive those fellows out of those woods." With his words echoing in their ears, the men of the 2nd plunged into the wood line at the double quick. Almost instantly their line was torn by the fire of Archer's men. As one soldier recalled, "The men around us began to fall rather promiscuously." In those first few moments it seemed as if a third of the regiment had fallen. Among those hit was Lt. Col. George H. Stevens, mortally wounded with a ball in his abdomen. Pvt. Emanuel Markle of Company B saw the man to his right go down, killed instantly, and a moment later a bullet smashed into his own shoe, lodging in his heel. As he laid there he heard Colonel Fairchild yell out, "Charge men, I mean charge," and the regiment surged deeper into the woods while bullets filled the air.

As the 2nd advanced into the woods, Reynolds knew they could not stem Archer's advance alone. Turning in his saddle to look for the rest of the brigade, a bullet struck him in the back of the head, and he fell to the ground. He

showed no visible wound, so at first his aide, Sgt. Charles H. Viel, believed he was
only stunned. Then, realizing the general was dead and fearing the body would
be captured should the attack fail, Viel found assistance and hurriedly carried
Reynold's body into town.

Men continued to fall. Sgt. Philo B. Wright, carrying the national colors, was
shot in both arms and the left thigh, but his life was spared when the bullet that
hit him in the chest was stopped by the socket of the color bearer's belt. Earlier
in the day, Pvt. Rasselas Davison, who had been in all of the regiment's fights,
told a friend that "the period of 'spoiling for a fight' had passed him." Seeing
the colors drop, he forgot his earlier pledge to avoid a fight, picked up the fallen
flag, and "bounded two rods to the front of the line and shouted for the boys
to come on." Davison would carry the colors of the 2nd for the rest of the war.
Moments later, Colonel Fairchild was hit, a bullet shattering his elbow. With no
direction, the regiment still continued forward, borne by its own momentum.

Faced with such enthusiasm and realizing that the rest of the Iron Brigade
was sweeping around their own exposed flank, Archer's men fell back. In their
retreat they left several hundred men and General Archer as captives. With
this, the concentration of the army Reynolds had hoped for occurred, but the
price had been high. Reynolds himself was dead, and when the roll was called at
Willoughby Run, 116 men of the 2nd were no longer in its ranks. The brigade
would fight again that afternoon and grudgingly give ground to the Seminary,
finally falling back through the town. At day's end, when the roll was taken on
Culp's Hill, only 45 weary but undefeated men would remain of the 302 who had
responded to Reynolds's call to "drive those fellows out."

MARC STORCH AND BETH STORCH have focused their work on the soldiers of
their native state of Wisconsin and have written a history of the 2nd Wisconsin
Volunteer Infantry, along with other essays and articles on the men of the Iron
Brigade. They are active in preservation, particularly in the Wilderness and South
Mountain, and helped found a group to preserve and renovate the Iron Brigade
monuments at Gettysburg.

The Unconquered

1st Tennessee Color Bearer

EARLY ON THE MORNING OF JULY 1, Gen. Henry Heth started his division from around Cashtown toward Gettysburg to find a much-needed supply of shoes. The battle-hardened brigade of Gen. James J. Archer's Tennessee and Alabama troops would lead the way.

After marching about three miles, Archer's column discovered Federal cavalry in a field to their right front. The 5th Alabama Battalion marching at the front of the brigade, and two companies of the 13th Alabama, were ordered out to form a skirmish line. The order for the colors to be uncased was given, and the brigade moved forward on the road in column; the cavalry fell back and exchanged fire with the gray-clad skirmishers.

Driving the Federals back within about a mile and a half of Gettysburg, Archer found Gamble's dismounted cavalry drawn up across the Chambersburg Pike. Confederate artillery was put into position and opened fire on the Federals.

Archer's brigade, marching in columns of four to the right of the road, halted and faced left into the line of battle and was ordered to load. Deployed from left to right were the 7th Tennessee, 14th Tennessee, 1st Tennessee, and 13th Alabama.

About nine o'clock, the order "Forward" was passed down, and the gray line advanced as Federal shells fell among them, right of the line. Lt. John Calef, commanding Company A, 2nd U.S. Artillery, closely watched the Rebel advance, remarking that their battle flags looked redder and bloodier than he had seen them before. Calef ordered his gunners to aim at the Confederate flags. Escaping artillery fire by advancing down a gradual slope into a valley and driving the dismounted cavalry away, the 1st Tennessee and 13th Alabama shifted right to silence the Federal guns. Crossing a clear stream about three feet wide and knee-deep, the 1st

Tennessee advanced through a copse of trees running up a ravine. Spreading out in a fan as they neared the top of the ridge, they encountered the 7th Wisconsin of the Iron Brigade, and a vicious fight erupted. As the Black Hats charged them in column, the Tennesseans laid on their backs to load and whirled over to fire. The fight lasted about thirty minutes until the 19th Indiana hit the 1st Tennessee on its right flank. The order was given to fall back. The Tennessee boys fell back across the creek with Federals all around them, and a number were captured.

William Murray of the 19th Indiana reported, "The Tennessee color bearer broke through the lines and run up a slope, and then turned and shook the flag at our troops and disappeared from sight." Murray shot at the Rebel twice, as did others eager to capture a Confederate flag, but the Tennessean eluded his pursuers and escaped.

The 1st Tennessee color bearer was Wiley Woods of Company F, "The Salem Invincibles." Woods also was the man in the Pickett-Pettigrew charge on July 3 who took his regiment's colors to the stone wall at the Angle, where he and the flag were captured.

BOB PARKER, a Civil War scholar, has done extensive research on the life of the Confederate soldier, inspired by listening to his great-uncle tell stories he had heard from his father, a Confederate soldier. He has also contributed to the A&E series *Civil War Journal.*

The Fight for the Colors

THE EARLY MORNING SKIRMISHING WAS OVER. NOW LEE'S ARMY OF Northern Virginia was facing those veteran foot soldiers of John F. Reynolds's Union I Corps on the fields of the McPherson and Wills farms west of Gettysburg. The right of Cutler's brigade, the first Yankee infantry to deploy that morning of July 1, 1863, was the first to suffer from the hammer blow of Davis's Mississippi and North Carolina infantrymen, and had to withdraw to the cover of the woods. The last to abandon their positions were the 147th New York and Hall's 1st Maine Battery, and they paid bitterly for their tenacity. The New York regiment lost over 70 percent of their fighting force, and Hall was compelled to leave behind one of his 3-inch rifles when the team taking it off was shot and bayoneted by Davis's attacking vanguard.

It seemed as if Davis's victorious force would have unimpeded access to the right and rear of Meredith's Iron Brigade, who were in the Herbst Woods contesting the advance of Archer, and would thus seal the fate of the only part of the I Corps then on the field. But Lt. Col. Rufus Dawes, commanding the 6th Wisconsin, had already started his regiment toward the head of Davis's advancing line from his position as division reserve. Joined by the 95th New York and 14th Brooklyn at the fencing paralleling the Chambersburg Pike, all three regiments received Dawes's command: "Forward, charge!"

Disorganized by its headlong and spirited attack, Davis's brigade was forced to fall back to the protection of a railroad cut, and his men jumbled together along the line of the unfinished railroad grade. Where the slopes of the cut were either nonexistent or not so deep, the Southern muskets blazed into the ranks of the advancing Wisconsin line. In the 130 yards between the pike and the railroad grade, the 6th Wisconsin lost 175 men—more than one man for each yard gained.

Soon the drama approached its climax. Where the cut was deep, the Confederates were totally at the mercy of the Yankees standing above them with muskets aiming into their midst, and most saw the wisdom of a hasty surrender. On the Confederate left, however, where the cut was not a factor, the fighting continued for a few minutes more.

Inspired by their many losses, several men of the 6th Wisconsin tried to seize the battle flag of the 2nd Mississippi while it waved defiantly from the railroad grade. At least a dozen of Dawes's men fell beside those of the Mississippi color guard, the Wisconsin soldiers eager to take the flag and avenge the loss of so many comrades. The Mississippians were defiant and desperate to protect the flag carried on so many glorious battlefields. Finally, it was a personal contest between the color-bearer W. B. Murphy and Corp. Francis A. Waller of the 6th Wisconsin.

Hoping to tear the flag from its staff to prevent its capture, Murphy was ultimately foiled when he and the flagstaff were seized by Corporal Waller. The force of Waller's strong grasp and determined look, the sounds of surrendering comrades in the cut, and the moans of so many of the color guard lying about him convinced Murphy that he must either yield the colors or his life. There would soon be none to protect them.

With the Confederate defeat at the railroad grade, the 6th Wisconsin and the New Yorkers saved the Iron Brigade from certain envelopment, and thus ensured its victory over Archer. The repulse of Archer and Davis delayed the Confederate renewal of the attack and provided the time needed to bring up the remainder of the I Corps. Ultimately, both commanders would be committed to a battle. The action at the railroad cut provided that moment when what could have been a mere morning skirmish became the historic battle of Gettysburg.

KATHLEEN GOERG HARRISON has been a historian at Gettysburg National Military Park since 1976; she currently serves in that capacity and as cultural resources specialist. She is the author of *Nothing but Glory: Pickett's Division at Gettysburg*, as well as numerous articles on the battle.

The Boy Colonel

IT WAS TWO O'CLOCK ON THE AFTERNOON OF JULY 1, 1863. SINCE THE INITIAL clash that morning, the fighting north and west of Gettysburg had intensified until now every soldier knew a great battle was at hand. Robert E. Lee's Army of Northern Virginia was on the offensive, and fresh troops were moving forward to drive their blue-clad foes from ridgelines that commanded the town beyond.

No officer felt the urgency of the hour more keenly than Col. Henry King Burgwyn Jr., commander of the 26th North Carolina. His was one of four North Carolina regiments in Brig. Gen. J. Johnston Pettigrew's brigade, which since noon had been waiting to enter the fray. Yankee shells and occasional spatters of musketry had been striking Burgwyn's position on Herr's Ridge, and the colonel was chafing at the bit. Now at last the time had come. Burgwyn called his men to attention, drew his sword, and took position on foot at the center of the regiment, ready to lead them forward.

Burgwyn's zeal was fueled by the impetuosity of youth; at twenty-one he was the youngest colonel in Lee's army, having risen to field grade while still in his teens. But Harry Burgwyn was something more than a "boy colonel." In two years of war he had forged a reputation as a firm disciplinarian, skilled drillmaster, and unsurpassed leader of men.

Born in Massachusetts and raised on a North Carolina plantation, Burgwyn had graduated from the University of North Carolina, then entered the Virginia Military Institute with the class of 1861. He ranked high as a scholar in both schools, and shortly after the outbreak of war was elected lieutenant colonel of the 26th North Carolina, a regiment commanded by future governor Zebulon B. Vance. "Zeb" Vance proved a better politician than officer, and it was Burgwyn who turned the enthusiastic but independent young Tar Heels into soldiers. At first he was viewed as something of a martinet, but by August 1862 when he succeeded Vance as colonel of the 26th, Burgwyn had won his men's affection as well as their respect.

In the two years prior to Gettysburg, Burgwyn had been given scant opportunity to exercise his skills. His regiment had been stationed in a succession of military backwaters: on the Carolina coast, in the defenses of Richmond, and in southeast Virginia. At last, in May 1863, Pettigrew's brigade was assigned to Lee's army and joined in the second great invasion of the North. The men of the 26th North Carolina were ready and eager for the test. Well-uniformed and equipped, the unit mustered nearly full regimental strength; as Burgwyn reported, "I now command nearly as many men as most of our Brigadier Generals."

Yet as the Army of Northern Virginia marched on into Maryland and Pennsylvania, the men noticed that their young commander was uncharacteristically depressed. Some thought he had a premonition of approaching death. "God alone knows how tired I am of this war," Burgwyn had written his family. "I am sure that no day in my life will be ailed by me with the same degree of delight as that on which I hear the blessed tidings of peace assured."

Whatever his forebodings, the boy colonel advanced bravely into the holocaust of the first day's fight at Gettysburg. "His eye was aflame with the ardor of battle," recalled his second in command, Lt. Col. John R. Lane. "At the command Forward March," the nearly 900 soldiers in the 26th North Carolina "to a man stepped off apparently as willingly and as proudly as if they were on review." Opposing them were some of the finest troops in the Union Army: the tough westerners of the Iron Brigade.

Men struck down at every step, the 26th North Carolina swept on toward the enemy position on McPherson Ridge. Their ranks were disordered by the tangled briars and undergrowth that bordered Willoughby Run, but under heavy fire the men splashed across and re-formed on the opposite bank. Already four soldiers had fallen while bearing the regimental battle flag—a newly issued banner whose folds were now torn with bullets. "Yelling like demons," the Tar Heels charged uphill, driving the 24th Michigan and a portion of the 19th Indiana into the shelter of the McPherson Woods.

There the Yankees stood their ground. Staggered by the hail of flying lead, the Confederate line halted and opened fire on their antagonists at a range of twenty yards. A deadly slugging match ensued. Gen. Henry Heth would later note that the dead of Burgwn's regiment "marked his line of battle with the accuracy of a line at dress parade." The survivors continuously closed up on their colors; four more times the flag was shot down and instantly raised again.

In the thick of the fighting Capt. W. W. McCreery galloped up to Colonel Burgwyn with a message from General Pettigrew: "Your regiment has covered itself with glory today!" Then, leaping from his horse, McCreery picked up the banner and fell, shot through the heart. Second Lt. George Wilcox pulled the flag from under McCreery's body, stood up, and was bowled over.

Now Burgwyn himself snatched up the flag from a heap of fallen men. Seeing that the color company and those on its flanks were all but annihilated, he bore the colors to 1st Lt. Thomas Cureton of Company B and asked if he could furnish a man to carry them. Pvt. Frank Hunneycut stepped forward, took the flag, and went down.

Again Burgwyn raised the bloodstained banner. Bullets tore at his clothes and struck the scabbard that hung at his side. Pointing his sword at the enemy line, he turned to his embattled soldiers and urged them forward. At that moment a bullet ripped through both his lungs, and Burgwyn went down, the flag enfolding him as he fell.

Lieutenant Colonel Lane ran to the side of his stricken commander and at once saw that the wound was mortal. Then, with the words "It is my time to take them now," Lane snatched the bullet-riddled flag from the hand of its thirteenth bearer and led the regiment on.

At last the ravaged Yankee line fell back through McPherson's woods. As the Tar Heels followed in their wake, Lane was shot through the back of the head, the bullet emerging from his open mouth. For the final time that day the flag went down.

Lane would live to fight another day, but at least 95 soldiers of the 26th North Carolina had died in the charge. Another blooding on the third day of the battle depleted the ranks still further. Of 895 men who had begun the fight at Gettysburg, only 3 officers and 67 men remained present for duty. The regiment's total loss was a staggering 697; of these, 174 were killed outright or later died of wounds.

For two hours Burgwyn's life ebbed away as he lay in the arms of Lt. J. J. Young. He left messages of love for his family and words of praise for his men. Just before the end, the boy colonel's mind drifted back to the eve of battle, and he whispered, "I know my gallant Regiment will do their duty . . . where is my sword?"

BRIAN C. POHANKA has held editorial positions with several history magazines and was a senior researcher and writer on Time-Life Books' twenty-seven-volume history of the Civil War. A member of the Company of Military Historians, he serves in the ranks of the 5th New York Zouaves, a Civil War living history unit, and works to preserve the threatened legacy of Civil War sites.

Generals Robert E. Lee and A. P. Hill

Gettysburg Campaign, 1863

THE CONFEDERATE ARMY THAT MARCHED north into Pennsylvania in June 1863 was full of confidence and hope. At their head rode a man who, for many, had become a living legend—Robert E. Lee. With him was one of his most trusted lieutenants, Ambrose Powell Hill, commanding the Army of Northern Virginia's newly formed III Corps.

The uniforms worn by these men during the fateful days were in indicative of the self-confidence earned by two years of war. Those who saw General Lee invariably commented on his well-groomed, neat appearance. As he had his personal baggage with him, many daily clothing options were at his disposal. One staff officer, G. Moxley Sorrell, observed that Lee rarely carried a sword but always had binoculars by his side. On the march during the Gettysburg campaign, a soldier of the 17th Mississippi remembered that "he wore a long linen duster which so enveloped his uniform as to make it invisible." The image was further enhanced by a "broad brimmed straw hat, evidently the art of his many lady admirers." An account in the *Harrisburg Daily Patriot* described him as wearing "a heavy over-coat with a large cape and a black felt hat." Another witness, quoted in *Gettysburg Sources*, commented that on July 1 he was "plain and neat in his uniform of gray. Hat of gray felt with medium brim and boots fitted neatly coming to his knee with a border of fair leather an inch wide." Lee's unadorned style was perhaps more of a surprise to those who were not close to him, nor even in the same army. Hospital steward Henry F. Miller, Company D, 142nd Pennsylvania Volunteers, while attending wounded behind Confederate lines at Gettysburg on July 3, 1863, wrote in his diary that "General Lee and several of his Staff Officers were in the Hospital this morning. Lee was

dressed like a citizen without any side arms." Lt. Col. Arthur J. L. Fremantle commented on Lee at Gettysburg, "He generally wears a long grey jacket, a high black felt hat, and blue trousers tucked into his Wellington boot. I never saw him carry arms; and the only mark of his military rank are the three stars on his collar." Contradicting others about the sword, Gen. John Bell Hood reminisced that on the morning of July 2, "General Lee with his coat buttoned to the throat, sabre belt around his waist and field glasses pending at his side walked up and down in the shade of large trees near us." Lt. J. Winder Laird, who saw the great commander nearly a year later, remarked in his diary on the general's plain dress and noted that while mounted, "he carried a bush in his hand with which he brushed flies from his horse."

One of Lee's most able subordinates, Gen. Ambrose Powell Hill, has been inaccurately characterized by modern writers as wearing a bright red battle shirt throughout the entire war. General Hill, in the heat of summer during the 1862 Peninsula campaign, sometimes wore a red-and-black striped shirt and, when on the march, an unadorned "hunting shirt" without insignia of rank. However, the uniform he wore more often on campaign, "a Fatigue jacket of gray flannel, his felt hat slouched over his noble brow," and hip-length boots, must have seemed more appropriate attire. In the battle that lay ahead, the officer's sack coat, with general's rank plainly visible, would forestall any question of authority. This would be important when commanding troops in the newly formed corps—troops who may not yet know him on sight. In addition, unlike General Lee, and perhaps some other Army of Northern Virginia officers, General Hill most always wore his sword, according to British military observer Lt. Col. Arthur J. L. Fremantle.

EARL J. COATES is a lifelong student of the American Civil War, specializing in arms and uniforms, and has contributed to and published numerous articles and books on the subject. He served for more than thirty years with the National Security Agency and was the first curator of the agency's National Cryptologic Museum. He helped form the Friends of the National Parks at Gettysburg, serving for over six years as its president, and has been a proud member of the Company of Military Historians since 1962.

Iron Brigade, 24th Michigan Volunteers

July 1, 1863

THE MEN AND BOYS OF THE 24TH MICHIGAN VOLUNTEER INFANTRY marched to Gettysburg in 1863 with new black hats and something to prove. They were just ten months in service. The regiment was formed in the summer of 1862 in a wave of patriotism that swept Wayne County after secessionists and Confederate agents disrupted a Union rally at Detroit. When the 24th Michigan reached Washington, it was assigned to one of the best fighting organizations of the Army of the Potomac, the Iron Brigade of the West. The brigade was famous for the tall black hats worn by the soldiers (the Model 1858 dress issue for the U.S. regulars) and because it was the only all-western unit in the eastern armies. The Michigan newcomers in their caps and bright new uniforms were given a cool reception. The four original regiments, the 2nd, 6th, and 7th Wisconsin and 19th Indiana, now totaled just about the same as the arriving reinforcements. The colonel of the Michigan men was Judge Henry Morrow, a native of Virginia who saw service in Mexico as a young man and had come West to make a name for himself. He was proud of his volunteers and extolled the qualities of his new regiment in a speech to the assembled brigade, only to be met with cold silence.

The famous brigade and its new regiment saw only limited service at Fredericksburg, where the Wolverines came under their first artillery fire. "Steady men," Morrow called out at one point, "those Wisconsin men are watching you." In the Chancellorsville campaign, there was a spirited river crossing, but not the kind of fighting endured earlier by the Iron Brigade at Antietam or before the stone wall at South Mountain. The Michigan regiment's coveted black hats arrived in May 1863, and one of the Michigan men reported, "They made our appearance, like the name of the brigade, quite unique." But it was on the opening day of the battle of Gettysburg, July 1, 1863, that the 24th Michigan won a share of the Iron Brigade's reputation.

The brigade was with the first Federal infantry thrown into the fighting northwest of the town. "Look there," the Johnnies call on seeing Iron Brigade regiments deploying, "it is those damned black-hatted devils." With the 6th Wisconsin held in reserve, the four regiments charge an advancing Confederate brigade in the woods south of the Chambersburg Pike, capturing men and flags, then pull back to a defensive position along the east edge of Willoughby Run. The Confederates come again in the afternoon with loud yells, and within minutes the entire Union line, the Iron Brigade in a key position on McPherson Ridge, is in trouble. Flanked on the left and right, the four western regiments make one stand, then another, and then a third, often firing into the very faces of the pressing Confederates. There is a fourth and a fifth rally and finally a last-ditch stand by the Black Hats with their backs to the Lutheran Seminary building. Of the 499 Michigan men who marched to Gettysburg, only 100 remain on the firing line.

Morrow is seemingly everywhere in the swirl of bullets and smoke; finally, the last of his color guard dead, he takes up the tattered flag of his regiment. A private steps up, takes the banner, and is shot down. Morrow again raises the flag, waving it, only to be struck by a glancing bullet that rips his scalp and leaves him half-blind with pain and blood. Lt. George Hutton drags his stunned and raging colonel from the line and helps him back to the town and medical assistance. Behind them, the Federal line is being swept away by the surging Confederate advance.

The Iron Brigade is almost destroyed in the day of fighting. Of the 1,883 men on the roster, only 491 are in ranks when, at dusk on July 2, a quartermaster sergeant passes out rations on Culp's Hill. But the hours bought with hard fighting by the westerners allow the Union army to rally on a new defensive position on Cemetery Ridge. It is that line that proves decisive in the Union victory over the next two days. Of all the brigades, the Iron Brigade has the highest loss, at 65 percent. The largest number of casualties in any regiment in the brigade, indeed, of any regiment at Gettysburg, occurs in the 24th Michigan. Of the 496 Michigan men, 79 are killed, 237 wounded, and 83 missing.

LANCE J. HERDEGEN is the former director of the Institute for Civil War Studies at Carroll University and works as historical consultant for the Civil War Museum of the Upper Middle West at Kenosha, Wisconsin. He is the author of several books about the Civil War, including *The Men Stood Like Iron: How the Iron Brigade Won Its Name* and *Those Damned Black Hats! The Iron Brigade in the Gettysburg Campaign.*

The Black Hats

19th Indiana Regiment, Iron Brigade

THE 19TH INDIANA MARCHED TO PENNSYLVANIA IN 1863 AS A VETERAN regiment in the famous Iron Brigade. Along with the 2nd, 6th, and 7th Wisconsin, and later the 24th Michigan, the Hoosiers saw action at Gainesville, Second Bull Run, South Mountain, Antietam, Fredericksburg, and Chancellorsville. None of the fighting, the veterans said later, prepared them for what they called the "four long hours" of July 1, 1863, at Gettysburg, where the Iron Brigade was all but wrecked.

The brigade ran into the infantry fighting at midmorning on a hot day and enjoyed early success in the open fields northwest of Gettysburg, knocking back two Confederate brigades. "It's those damned Black Hats!" the Confederate called upon seeing the western men and their famous headgear. By afternoon, however, the Confederates were advancing in heavy lines to seize the town. The Iron Brigade was strung out in a defensive position above Willoughby Run on McPherson Ridge. The 19th Indiana was on the left with the 24th Michigan, 7th Wisconsin, and 2nd Wisconsin extending the line to the north. The 6th Wisconsin was detached and posted elsewhere. The Union line was outnumbered and overlapped.

By midafternoon, the outnumbered Hoosiers were fighting for their lives, bending back under heavy flank fire and disappearing "like dew before the morning sun." The 19th Indiana carried two flags—a blue regimental presented by the ladies of Indianapolis and a national color requisitioned when a complementary national flag from 1861 was retired. Sgt. Burlington Cunningham, already once wounded, was carrying the national banner when hit a second time. Nearby, Color Corp. Abe Buckles also went down. Lt. Col. William Dudley grabbed the national flag and was shot in the right shin—a wound that would cost him his leg. In the noise and smoke, Sgt. Maj. Asa Blanchard came up to take the flag, saying: "Colonel, you shouldn't have done this. That was my duty. I shall never forgive myself for letting you touch that flag." Eight Indiana color bearers were now down, and half the regiment killed or wounded.

Under heavy fire from two advancing Confederate brigades, the Indiana flag—now in the hands of another man—fell yet again. Before Blanchard could reach it, however, Color Corp. David Phipps, who was carrying the Indiana regimental, scooped up the fallen national and was waving it with one hand. Then Phipps was wounded and fell on both flags. "The flag is down!" someone shouted, and Capt. William W. Macy yelled to a nearby private to "Go and get it!" "Go to hell, I won't do it," said the soldier.

Macy, Lt. Crockett East, and Color Corp. Burr Clifford rolled Phipps off the flags. Aware the bright silk was attracting bullets, East furled the banner, got it into its case, and was trying to wrap the tassels when he was shot and killed. Macy and Clifford finally got the two flags in the cases only to be confronted by an angry Blanchard, who demanded the flags. "No, there's been enough men shot down with it," said Macy, but Blanchard appealed to Col. Samuel J. Williams, and the colonel told Macy to turn over the flags. In a swirl of bullets, Blanchard stubbornly unfurled the national colors and tied the case around his waist, calling in a loud voice, "Rally boys!" He was waving it when a bullet severed an artery in his thigh and he fell in a gush of blood, dying almost immediately. Clifford then picked up the banner and made a run for the town and safety.

The Iron Brigade line was soon swept away, and the surviving Black Hats made their way through Gettysburg to the Federal rally point on Cemetery Hill. Their stout fighting delayed the Confederates long enough to allow Union forces to secure the defensive positions that would win the battle over the next two days. But the holding action came at terrible cost. The Iron Brigade marched to Gettysburg with 1,883 men, and by dusk only 671 rallied around the flags. In the 19th Indiana, of the 288 carried into the fight, only 78 were still in ranks—a loss of almost 73 percent.

LANCE J. HERDEGEN is the former director of the Institute for Civil War Studies at Carroll University and works as historical consultant for the Civil War Museum of the Upper Middle West at Kenosha, Wisconsin. He is the author of several books about the Civil War, including *The Men Stood Like Iron: How the Iron Brigade Won Its Name* and *Those Damned Black Hats! The Iron Brigade in the Gettysburg Campaign.*

General J. B. Gordon at Gettysburg

J ULY 1, 1863, UNFOLDED IN THE OUTSKIRTS OF GETTYSBURG ABOUT AS
well as any Confederate could have hoped. Although, in hindsight, events
of the next two days tend to overshadow July 1, that day might be adjudged
among the most successful in the annals of the Army of Northern Virginia.

Confederates concentrating toward Gettysburg from points north and west
arrived in timely fashion and unhinged a succession of Federal positions. As the

division under Robert E. Rodes cleared Oak Ridge, Jubal A. Early's division fell upon the exposed Union XI Corps, on lower ground to the east, and drove it back into town. The six Georgia regiments of Gordon's brigade played a key role in that triumphant advance.

Brig. Gen. John Brown Gordon had come to the Civil War without the military education and experience that prepared so many of his contemporaries for their dreadful responsibilities in mortal combat. His intelligence, leadership qualities, and bravery combined to make Gordon stand out as the best of R. E. Lee's high-ranking officers without a professional prewar background.

When Gordon and his hard-bitten veteran Georgian infantrymen approached the Northern position on July 1, they discovered that it stretched across a prominent knoll near the Blocher farmhouse and barn. As they aligned to attack, the Confederates came upon the willow-lined course of Rock Creek, meandering between them and their foe.

John Gordon's ramrod military posture and clarion voice had made him a familiar focus for his brigade's attention on many a battlefield by the middle of 1863. On July 1 he bestrode a striking horse that heightened his profile. His men had captured the "huge black horse . . . handsomely caparisoned" from Federal general Robert H. Milroy at Winchester a fortnight earlier. The "immense" creature "of unusually fine proportions" made a "magnificent appearance" as Gordon rode him toward Rock Creek. Although cannon fire did not bother the beautiful mount, he later proved terrified of musketry—but at Gettysburg as the general and his new horse approached battle, they were the cynosure of every eye.

An artillerist who watched Gordon trot forward marveled at the black horse: "He must have been a direct descendant of . . . Bucephalus. . . . I never saw a horse's neck so arched, his eye so fierce, his nostril so dilated." The general's demeanor impressed the same observer: "Gordon was the most glorious and inspiring thing I ever looked upon. . . . Bareheaded, hat in hand, arms extended, and in a voice like a trumpet, exhorting his men. It was superb; absolutely thrilling."

Col. Clement A. Evans, who eventually would succeed Gordon in brigade command, reported on the same scene: "Gordon rode superbly that day . . . among and ever near the heroic men in the advancing line, and his bearing was every inch the incarnate spirit of chivalry."

The Georgians moved briskly out of the Rock Creek bottom and swarmed over the heavily defended knoll. Beyond the crest, Gordon ran across a badly wounded enemy, Brig. Gen. Francis C. Barlow. Their encounter became one of the famous small episodes of Gettysburg, generating controversy that continues today.

A staff officer at Confederate II Corps headquarters called Gordon's attack "one of the most warlike & animated spectacles I ever looked on." Gordon himself recounted the success in a letter to his wife written on July 7: "We charged the heavy lines of the Enemy & had a desperate fight. I consider the action of the Brigade as brilliant as any charge of the war—and it is so regarded by the officers of the army. . . . It surpassed anything I have seen during the war."

Six days after the stirring scenes near Rock Creek, a captain in Gordon's brigade wrote home and described how the general shouted to his victorious men: "'You are the finest Troops that ever were led into a fight.' We replied, 'You are the best Genl who ever led men into a fight.'"

ROBERT K. KRICK was the chief historian of Fredericksburg National Park for thirty years. He is the author of numerous books and articles about the Civil War, including *The Smoothbore Volley That Doomed the Confederacy* and *Conquering the Valley*.

Cemetery Hill

THE MORNING OF JULY 1, 1863, WAS FRUSTRATING FOR MAJ. GEN. George G. Meade, who commanded the Army of the Potomac. He had issued a circular to his corps commanders with details of his plan to fight a defensive battle behind Pipe Creek, Maryland. But then, about 11:30 A.M. a message arrived from Maj Gen. John F. Reynolds, reporting that his I Corps was engaging the enemy at Gettysburg. Another message from Brig. Gen. John Buford, commanding the 1st Division of the Cavalry Corps, also reported the Confederate advance.

At 1:00 P.M., one of Reynolds's aides arrived to report that the general had been killed. That was enough for Meade. Something now had to be done, and he needed better information about what was happening at Gettysburg. With his chief of staff—Daniel Butterfield—Meade, headquartered at Taneytown, Maryland, rode over to the nearby camps of the II Army Corps.

Maj. Gen. Winfield Scott Hancock led the corps. Aged thirty-nine, Hancock had been promoted to corps command on May 22 and was the most junior corps commander in the Army of the Potomac except for Sykes of the 5th, promoted when Meade assumed army command three days before. Meade and Butterfield appeared in Hancock's tent and briefed the general on the situation at Gettysburg. Meade did not want to go to the battlefield because he needed to be in a central location to coordinate the army's movements as the situation became better known. The general wanted someone he trusted in charge of the battlefield.

Therefore, Meade ordered Hancock to go to Gettysburg and assume command of the I and XI Army Corps, known to be at Gettysburg, and also the III Corps, stationed nearby at Emmitsburg. "If you think the ground and position there a better one to fight a battle under existing circumstances, you will so advise the general, and he will order all the troops up."

Hancock at first protested. Both Maj. Gen. Oliver O. Howard, commanding the XI Army Corps, and Maj. Gen. Daniel Sickles of the III Corps outranked him. Meade told Hancock that the War Department had given him latitude to appoint any general to any command, regardless of rank or seniority.

Taneytown was thirteen miles from Gettysburg. Hancock and some aides left for Gettysburg in the back of an ambulance so they could study regional maps before they arrived. The officers then mounted and rode the remaining distance.

General Hancock arrived on Cemetery Hill about 3:30 P.M., as survivors of the I and XI Army Corps were streaming back through the town to the hill. Everywhere he looked, Hancock saw fragments of regiments and batteries coming south, followed by Confederates in the distance.

What happened in the next few minutes has been the subject of controversy. Hancock immediately sought out General Howard, who was desperately attempting to rally fugitives of the two corps. The two officers met near the cemetery gatehouse. Hancock told a startled Howard that Meade had sent him to Gettysburg to assume command of the troops on the field. Howard told Hancock that he was the senior general present.

"I am aware of that, general, but I have written orders in my pocket from General Meade, which I will show you if you wish to see them," said Hancock.

Howard replied. "No, I do not doubt your word, General Hancock, but you can give no orders here while I am here."

"Very well, General Howard, I will second any order that you have to give, but General Meade has also directed me to select a field on which to fight this battle."

Hancock then looked around and observed the terrain. The general liked what he saw and told Howard that the position at Gettysburg was the "strongest position by nature upon which to fight a battle" that he had ever seen. If Howard approved, continued Hancock, he would select Gettysburg as the battlefield. When Howard replied in the affirmative, Hancock exclaimed, "Very well, sir, I select this as the battlefield."

Hancock and Howard, together with Maj. Gen. Abner Doubleday of the I Army Corps, set about to position the retreating troops. Hancock's presence alone was worth thousands of men. Lt. Edward N. Whittier of the 5th Maine Battery never forgot Hancock's "commanding, controlling presence, nor the fresh courage he imparted." On this day, Hancock lived up to his "superb" cognomen he had received a year before. He acted with great calmness and authority, and the defeated soldiers who saw Hancock rallied. Soon, a semblance of order appeared along the Union lines.

Hancock ordered Doubleday to send a regiment to occupy Culp's Hill. Doubleday at first hesitated; his corps was shot to pieces and the men were tired. But he obeyed and sent an entire division to occupy the hill. When the XII Army Corps approached the field, Hancock sent troops to occupy Little Round Top to protect the left flank. At 4:00 P.M., Hancock sent an aide back to Meade with his appraisal of the situation—Gettysburg was a good place to fight, and the units present would remain until dark to allow Meade time to decide.

At 5:25 P.M., Hancock sent a longer message to Meade, essentially repeating his first communication. Meade already had decided to concentrate the army at Gettysburg; Hancock's messages only reinforced Meade's decision. Largely due to Hancock's presence, the defeated troops had been rallied and placed in position to defy a further Rebel advance. He had selected the battlefield, and now the Army of the Potomac was coming to give battle on the morrow. The climax of the war was at hand.

DR. RICHARD A. SAUERS, a native of Lewisburg, Pennsylvania, received his MA and PhD in American history from the Pennsylvania State University. He is the author of numerous books, articles, introductions, and book reviews on various aspects of the Civil War, including *The Gettysburg Campaign, A Caspian Sea of Ink: The Meade-Sickles Controversy,* and *Advance the Colors! Pennsylvania Civil War Battleflags.*

Battle in the Streets

Baltimore Street, Gettysburg, July 1–3, 1863

T HE BATTLE OF GETTYSBURG CAUGHT HUNDREDS OF CIVILIANS—AND their homes—in the deadly crossfire of contending armies. Just as the Southern town of Fredericksburg had been ravaged by war, so the once-peaceful Pennsylvania village was transformed into a death-strewn battleground.

Following the collapse of the Federal I and XI Corps on July 1, Confederate troops established a foothold in the southern portion of the town from whence they could fire on the Union stronghold on Cemetery Hill. On July 2, the 73rd Pennsylvania regiment attempted to clear the Rebels from their positions, but the Georgia and Louisiana defenders were cleverly concealed and stymied the Federals with well-aimed shots. Firing from windows and rooftops, and from the cover of an improvised barricade on Baltimore Street, the Southern infantry easily repulsed the Yankees.

The deadly sniper's duel continued on July 3, and it was a stray bullet from the action that took the life of twenty-year-old Jennie Wade, the only Gettysburg civilian killed.

BRIAN C. POHANKA has held editorial positions with several history magazines and was a senior researcher and writer on Time-Life Books' twenty-seven-volume history of the Civil War. A member of the Company of Military Historians, he serves in the ranks of the 5th New York Zouaves, a Civil War living history unit, and works to preserve the threatened legacy of Civil War sites.

Decision at Dawn

G ENERAL ROBERT E. LEE FACED AN AGONIZING DECISION WHEN JULY 2,
1863, dawned hot and muggy. The previous day, units of his II and III
Corps had met Federal soldiers from two corps and had driven them
through Gettysburg to the heights south of town. Lee had desired to pursue the
broken enemy formations, but his subordinates, notably Richard S. Ewell, his II
Corps commander, failed to appreciate the circumstances and did not not follow
Lee's suggestion to press forward.

When night fell, Lee had been unsure of what to do. In response to Lt. Gen. James Longstreet's proposal for a flanking movement, Lee had replied, "If the enemy is there tomorrow, we must attack him." However, Lee sorely missed his cavalry chief, Jeb Stuart, who had been out of touch with the army for days. Without cavalry, Lee had lost the eyes of his army and had no firm understanding of either the terrain or of how many Yankees might be on or approaching the battlefield.

Longstreet, Lee's I Corps commander, was his most trusted subordinate now that Stonewall Jackson was dead. However, Longstreet expressed an unwillingness to attack what appeared to be a strong Union position. Lee sought the counsel of his II Corps officers and found them apprehensive to attack in their front. When Lee finally went to sleep after midnight, he was still in favor of an offensive battle but remained uncertain about what to do.

Thus, Lee was awake well before dawn. The general's headquarters were somewhere on the western slope of Seminary Ridge, between the Chambersburg Pike and the Lutheran Theological Seminary. Before dawn broke, Lee sent engineer Capt. Samuel R. Johnston with a small escort to scout the Federal left flank, of which little was known at that hour. Lee was thinking of an assault from that direction because Ewell appeared unwilling to attack Cemetery Hill and Culp's Hill on the Union right.

While Johnston was absent, Longstreet and some of his staff officers rode up and joined Lee, who was pacing up and down beside a fallen tree near his headquarters. Longstreet renewed his idea for a flanking movement, which Lee again rejected. Soon, Maj. Gen. John B. Hood, commanding Longstreet's leading division, arrived to report that his troops were en route and would soon be available for duty.

By that time, Lee and Longstreet had been joined by several other personalities. Lt. Gen. Ambrose P. Hill, commander of the III Corps, together with Maj. Gen. Henry Heth (one of his division commanders), joined the throng near Lee. Heth's division was stationed in the area and had been bloodied on July 1; Heth himself had been wounded in the head but survived because he had folded a newspaper as a liner for his too-large hat.

Ensconced in a nearby tree were two foreign officers observing Lee's army—English Lt. Col. James A. L. Fremantle of the Coldstream Guards and Capt. Justus Scheibert of the Prussian engineers. Fremantle trained his binoculars on the Federal position and kept informing those below of what he could see. Also on hand were Capt. Fitzgerald Ross, who was an Austrian hussar officer, and Francis Lawley, correspondent for the *Times* of London.

Hood arrived and joined Longstreet on the fallen tree; both men nervously whittled on sticks as Lee continued to pace. Hood recalled that Lee's coat was buttoned to the throat despite the warm morning, swordbelt buckled at his waist and binoculars dangling from his side. Lee "seemed full of hope, yet, at times buried deep in thought." Lee once paused and told Hood, "The enemy is there, and if we do not whip him, he will whip us."

Longstreet heard Lee's remark and took Hood aside, telling him, "The general is a little nervous this morning. He wishes me to attack. I do not wish to do so without Pickett. I never like to go into battle with one boot off." Longstreet referred to George Pickett's division, left behind to guard the rear in the absence of Stuart's troopers. Pickett was to be relieved and would rejoin the army later that day.

One can only guess at Lee's thoughts as he paced back and forth in front of his generals and their staff. Lee had not expected a battle so soon, but, once engaged, he gave no serious thought to retreating to a better position in the mountains west of Gettysburg or to adopt Longstreet's flanking proposal to force Meade to abandon his strong position. The battle was joined, and the outcome would be decided on this field. However, Lee's corps commanders did not eagerly accept their chief's plans, and on this day Lee was at a loss over how to coordinate the Army of Northern Virginia.

Captain Johnston later reported to Lee and told the general how vulnerable the Yankee left flank appeared to be. Based on Johnston's erroneous conclusions, Lee ordered Longstreet to take his corps and attack "up the Emmitsburg Road" while Ewell assaulted Culp's Hill. Hill's men would aid Longstreet and attack in their front if the opportunity presented itself. By day's end, new place-names would join the growing roster of Civil War sites: the Peach Orchard, Devil's Den, the Wheatfield, Little Round Top, Culp's Hill.

DR. RICHARD A. SAUERS, a native of Lewisburg, Pennsylvania, received his MA and PhD in American history from the Pennsylvania State University. He is the author of numerous books, articles, introductions, and book reviews on various aspects of the Civil War, including *The Gettysburg Campaign, A Caspian Sea of Ink: The Meade-Sickles Controversy,* and *Advance the Colors! Pennsylvania Civil War Battleflags.*

"The Men Must See Us Today"

MOMENTS BEFORE, ONE OF THE MOST DESTRUCTIVE AND PARALYZING volleys of the war was fired from the ranks of the 124th New York Infantry Regiment into the attacking 1st Texas Infantry, barely 200 feet distant. Now the entire front of the 124th New York is ablaze, the men firing at will from behind the four rifled guns of Smith's New York Battery at the stone wall enclosing the pasture that surrounded Devil's Den. The New Yorkers of Ward's brigade had been impatient for this moment of July 2, 1863, forced to watch most of the enemy's advance without firing, under orders of their colonel, Van Horne Ellis.

Ellis and his "Orange Blossoms," recently transferred to this division after their original division was reorganized in June, were eager to win the respect and trust of their new comrades. They were conspicuous as newcomers because they retained the old blue corps badge, not yet having the opportunity or honor to exchange it for the "red patch" of Kearny's old division. This battle, however, would earn the 124th New York the compliments of their superiors and peers and the right to display the red badge.

Colonel Ellis was keenly aware of his responsibilities in holding the south end of this ridge, in defending the battery, and in guiding his regiment to the glories that would win them the respect of their new division. He wanted his men to take advantage of their prominent and good defensive position as long as possible, inflicting terrible casualties on the Texans and making them die for every foot of ground over which they passed toward the guns. Ellis's subordinates, particularly Maj. James Cromwell, were eager to press their advantage immediately and to counterattack the determined and still-advancing Texas line. Twice Cromwell was refused permission to mount this counterattack. At last, the officers' mounts are brought up, and the young major takes to his horse over the objections of his friends, with the grim reply that "the men must see us today." Riding from his position at the left of the regiment, Cromwell finds his colonel in the rear of the color company and waits in anticipation, his eyes moving from Ellis to the ever-nearing enemy and back to his commander again. Bugler Ross also waits expectantly, preparing to sound his colonel's orders above the clamor of the battle when signaled to do so.

With the Confederates less than fifty feet away, and almost upon the guns, the 124th New York has reached a crisis. The battery has been useless for some time, unable to depress its guns sufficiently to fire down the slopes of the cleared field upon the attacking Texans, but its presence has defiantly goaded the Confederates to try to take the pieces. The "Orange Blossoms" and their firepower have slowed the enemy advance to almost a standstill. It is time for Ellis, seated calmly on his gray, to yield to the entreaties of Major Cromwell and allow the men to drive their weakening enemy from their front. The orders are given, and the men rush headlong down the slopes behind the mounted Cromwell, many following him to a death in front of the III Corps battle line. Before the counterattack is over, both Ellis and Cromwell will be felled, and the 124th will lose fearfully. But the Confederate advance on their front will be noticeably more hesitant to launch a new attack on Smith's guns, winning valuable time for the

Union army to reinforce the left flank against the attacks on Devil's Den and the Round Tops.

KATHLEEN GOERG HARRISON has been historian at Gettysburg National Military Park since 1976, and serves in that capacity and as cultural resources specialist. She is the author of *Nothing but Glory: Pickett's Division at Gettysburg*, as well as numerous articles on the battle.

Berdan's Sharpshooters

O N THE EVENING OF JULY 1, 1863, THE REGIMENTS OF THE ARMY OF THE
Potomac's III Corps arrived in Gettysburg and settled into bivouac
after a fatiguing forced march. That day had seen sharp fighting north
of Gettysburg as Confederate infantry clashed with Federals of the I and XI
Corps. Among the tired veteran soldiers to arrive in Gettysburg on the evening
of July 1 were Col. Hiram Berdan's 1st U.S. Sharpshooters and Lt. Col. Henry
Stoughton's 2nd U.S. Sharpshooters. Both regiments of elite marksmen were at
the time attached to Gen. David Birney's 1st Division after their previous stay in

Whipple's 3rd Division was ended in June following devastating losses at Chancellorsville. The morning of July 2 found Berdan's sharpshooters scattered across the Pennsylvania landscape in detachments by company and battalion. At the foot of Big Round Top, with their left flank companies staggered to the south of the Slyder farm and their left flank resting near Devil's Den, the 2nd Regiment bore the brunt of Col. William Oates's Alabamians. Companies D, E, F, and I of the 1st Regiment, as well as the 3rd Maine Infantry in reserve, under immediate command of Lt. Col. Caspar Trepp, were sent on a botched reconnaissance into Pitzer Woods. Here they encountered skirmishers from Brig. Gen. Cadmus Wilcox's brigade, massing in preparation for a direct assault of Gen. Daniel Sickle's III Corps. The remaining companies of the 1st U.S. Sharpshooters were posted in advance of the III Corps along the Emmitsburg Road and around the Peach Orchard. On July 3 both regiments laid in wait close to the center of the Federal line, observing Gen. George Pickett's advancing battle lines. While the Confederate Army of Northern Virginia made good their return to Virginia in late July, the sharpshooters later participated in several minor skirmishes.

Before the Chancellorsville campaign of May 1863, both sharpshooter regiments languished for several months in winter camp. This period of rest saw Berdan's men clothed in the distinctive green dress uniforms that provided them with such fame and notoriety in 1861. The sharpshooters' uniforms of the last quarter of 1862 were described by an inspecting officer "as being a nearly threadbare collection of whatever they could attain, with no two men attired exactly alike." To prepare for the summer campaign, on June 6, 1863, the distinctive dark-green frock coats were placed in storage, and common blue flannel fatigue blouses were issued in their place. Hard rubber buttons, readily available from the regimental sutler and from old spare clothing, were placed on the blouses by some men. Dark-green kersey trousers were newly issued, and dark-green forage caps still bearing the blue lozenge of the disbanded 3rd Division were retained. However, after their transfer into the 1st Division, some men provided themselves with the famous red "Kearny patch." Overcoats, spare clothing and blankets, and tall russet leather leggings issued in February of that year were likewise turned over to quartermasters prior to the summer campaign.

During the series of arduous forced marches into Pennsylvania, many of the sharpshooters discarded even more equipment. Inexperienced recruits tossed full knapsacks and blankets to the side of the road, choosing instead to share the blankets of their thriftier compatriots. Veterans and recruits alike, however, discarded the stamped brass breastplates of their infantry model .58-caliber cartridge box straps, possibly in an attempt at concealment while in battle. The previously rampant problems with enlisted men discarding their bayonets and scabbards had been corrected by this time under orders issued by the sharpshooters' veteran soldier-of-fortune, Lt. Col. Casper Trepp.

Though their trademark green frock coats, leggings, and fur-covered knapsacks were now gone, Berdan's sharpshooters entered the battle of Gettysburg no less a remarkable fighting force. The two regiments would lose a total of 130 officers and enlisted men killed, wounded, captured, and missing within two days of heavy fighting and an additional day of active skirmishing with the remaining Confederate forces. As with every other major combat action in which they were engaged, Berdan's sharpshooters suffered heavily, but they would go down in history as the elite skirmishers and light infantrymen of the Army of the Potomac.

EARL J. COATES is a lifelong student of the American Civil War, specializing in arms and uniforms, and has contributed to and published numerous articles and books on the subject. He served for more than thirty years with the National Security Agency and was the first curator of the agency's National Cryptologic Museum. He helped form the Friends of the National Parks at Gettysburg, serving for over six years as its president, and has been a proud member of the Company of Military Historians since 1962.

Confederate Sharpshooter

IN AN ARMY NOTED FOR DARING AND ABILITY, THE PROWESS OF THE
Confederate sharpshooters was legendary. They were perhaps the best-
trained troops fielded by either side during the Southern Confederacy's
bid for independence.

Sometimes portrayed as shadowy riflemen who picked off enemy officers and
soldiers at long range, the role of the Confederate sharpshooters was far more
complex. Not only were sharpshooters marksmen, but they were also used to
spearhead attacks, cover retreats, and engage in specialized operations. In reality,
the sharpshooters were light infantrymen with honed skills and élan that would
not be seen again until the rise of specialized units in the twentieth century.

The sharpshooters' mode of warfare was feared and misunderstood by both friend and foe. In an era when battles were fought by lines of soldiers volleying with leveled muskets, the specter of an unseen rifleman killing from a thousand yards away was terrifying. Captured sharpshooters were sometimes summarily executed, yet many Army of Northern Virginia sharpshooters proudly and defiantly wore distinctive cloth badges: sharpshooters from McComb's and other brigades wore a red cross, Archer's men wore a red quatrefoil, Wilcox's sharpshooters wore a red cross on their sleeves, McRae's sharpshooters were identified by a gold cross on the left sleeve, McGowan's men wore a red band diagonally across the left elbow surmounted by a red star, and Blackford's sharpshooters wore a red trefoil.

Sharpshooter Captain John D. Young of Scale's brigade recalled: "It was the fortune of the sharpshooters to experience all the romance and glamour of war. From the earliest opening of the battle to its tragic close, the ears of the sharpshooters were made familiar with the peculiar music of the rifle. A battalion was composed of one commandant, eight commissioned officers, ten non-commissioned officers, one hundred and sixty privates, four scouts and two buglers, specially selected and drafted from each brigade. These were divided into four companies. As it was a matter of the utmost importance that men should be chosen of tried courage and steadiness, who were good marksmen and possessed of the requisite self-confidence, great care and caution were exercised in the drafts. The company officers in the corps were equally set apart for their military reputations in respect to zeal, intelligence, and personal gallantry. As soon as the requisite number of men was obtained, the command was placed on an independent footing—reporting directly to brigade headquarters. Thus closely associated together, rank and file soon learned to know and rely upon each other. Still further to increase this confidence, the companies were subdivided into groups of fours. These groups messed and slept together, and were never separated in action save by casualties of disability and death. They were the elite of the army."

Extensively trained in skirmish drill, bayonet tactics, marksmanship, and range estimation, the men soon "became proficient in their drill and excellent shots. The drill was conducted by signals on the bugle as the line when deployed, was too extended to be reached by voice, or, when silence was the requisite, by the wave of the sword of the officer in command. The sharpshooters were armed with the improved Enfield rifle; the scouts with rifles of the Whitworth make with telescopic sights."

This detailed study shows three surviving members of a sharpshooter group. The rifleman in the foreground uses an English knapsack for a rest as he aims his horrifically accurate Whitworth .451 hexagonal-bore rifle equipped with a Davidson side-mounted telescopic sight. His team members carry iron-mounted .577 P60 "Enfield" army rifles and English accoutrements. While most sharpshooters carried Enfield rifles, some used "small bore" long-range military rifles such as the Kerr, Turner, or Nuthall. Sharpshooters also used specialized rifles such as the Jacobs or .577 "Volunteer" rifles that resembled Enfield army rifles. Military rifles were preferred because of their reliability, standard calibers, and ability to be fitted with a bayonet.

The sharpshooters provided each brigade of the Army of Northern Virginia with an elite body of skilled riflemen. They truly were, as Sharpshooter Captain Young stated, "a 'spike-head' of Toledo steel, which was not suffered to rust from disuse."

WILLIAM O. ADAMS JR. has collected and shot historical weapons for sixty years, specializing in Confederate and imported British arms. He is a fifty-year veteran of the North-South Skirmish Association and is a member of the New England Antique Arms Society, the Massachusetts Arms Collectors, the Company of Military Historians, the Sons of Confederate Veterans, the Confederate Stamp Alliance, the 34th Battalion Virginia Cavalry, the Federal Law Enforcement Officers Association, and the National Rifle Association. He is a veteran and a retired federal agent and has consulted on numerous works on Civil War arms.

Saving the Flag

July 2, 1863

THE BATTLE OF GETTYSBURG HAS LONG BEEN NOTED FOR ITS MANY individual episodes at heroism, valor, courage, and death. The names of many landmarks on the battlefield—Little Round Top, Devil's Den, Slaughter Pen, the Angle—still provoke the American imagination to thoughts of those sultry July days in 1863. But no site has inspired as much awe as the Wheatfield. This plot of wheat and pasture, comprising only about twenty acres of the Rose farm, has been invariably described as a "maelstrom" and a "whirlpool of death," where the lifeblood of regiment after regiment was spilled. And still there was not enough blood to quench the dry and thirsty wheat. Few remember singular examples of bravery, but all can recall with shock, horror, and grief the magnitude of loss, the desperation of the fighting, and the images evoked by the words "maelstrom" and "whirlpool of death."

Yet the Wheatfield action did have a history that revealed individual acts of personal courage. The opening stages on the second day of Gettysburg's battle, July 2, 1863, did not affect this grain-laden field. When Gen. Daniel Sickles moved his III Corps into a new position in the prenoon hours, the field was still lush and cattle casually grazed on the cool grass in the small pasture in its lower end. But the late afternoon brought with it the tramping of mighty hosts, which turned the heavy-laden crop into pulverized stubble and turned *a* wheat field into *the* Wheatfield. For here was one of the weakest parts of the Union battle line, protected only by a battery of guns from Winslow's New York Artillery and a thin line of skirmishers and sharpshooters. When the Confederate Army of Northern Virginia launched its attack against the Union left about four o'clock that afternoon, the noticeable gap in the Union line was quickly observed and just as quickly filled. Forces from other parts of the line held by the Union Army of the Potomac were rushed to the new front, reaching their destination just in time.

The battle here opened when parts of the brigades of Gens. George Anderson and Joseph Kershaw descended from the wooded ridge between the Rose farm buildings and the Wheatfield. Both brigades had sustained casualties from Union artillery fire as they crossed the Emmitsburg Road from their own battle line on Seminary-Warfield Ridge, and they were shocked by the unexpectedly strong opposition that faced them from the lower end of the Wheatfield. But sustained fighting at the edges of the field soon weakened the Union line and necessitated adding fresh units.

This was while the Confederate brigades were concerned about being outflanked on their right and left by growing pressure from II Corps reinforcements at the Loop and Rose Woods. A Union countercharge against their front drove the Confederates back to the far edge of the woods, as they were already reeling from the artillery fire and were being thrown into confusion by their own alignment. Col. Jacob Sweitzer's brigade, from the Union V Corps, was ordered into the Wheatfield from its position along the public road at the field's northern edge, to support this successful attack across the field of trampled grain and into the woods. Three regiments advanced in line, with the 4th Michigan Volunteers on its right flank. Before they were fairly across the field, however, the tables had turned. No longer was there a threat to the ranks of South Carolinians under General Kershaw, but an overwhelming force was soon upon the right end of Sweitzer's own line.

Wofford's brigade of Georgians, originally ordered to follow the brigade of Barksdale at the Peach Orchard, had moved instead into the Loop and into the woods along the western edge of the Wheatfield. Here they drove the last remnant of Union forces from the salient of the new Union line, and men of the Irish Brigade fled to the safety of Cemetery Ridge through the guns of Winslow's battery. Colonel Sweitzer believed these fleeing units had been relieved by other V Corps infantrymen and did not suspect that Confederates now occupied the woods, even after several shots fell among his men from that direction. Believing these were gunshots from Union forces attempting to fire over and beyond Sweitzer and into the woods at Anderson's Georgians, the brigade continued on, deeper into the lowest part of the Wheatfield. Here, in the apex of the triangular pasture, they first realized the trap. A soldier remarked to an astonished Sweitzer: "Colonel, I'll be damned if I don't think we are faced the wrong way; the rebs are up there in the woods behind us, on the right." As if to verify it, men of the 4th Michigan began to fall with balls entering their bodies from two and sometimes three directions. Orders were hastily given to meet the new threat, but it was too late. The swelling battle line of Gen. W. T. Wofford was pouring out of the woods on the western edge of the Wheatfield, sweeping everything in its path. Some regiments of Kershaw's brigade fell in with the Georgians, and this mingled mass of Southerners, excited and drunk with victory, fell on the ranks of the exposed 4th Michigan.

Sweitzer's center and left barely had time to escape, but the men of the 4th Michigan were under peril of total envelopment. This was what the soldier feared most—to have his rear and flanks exposed to enemy fire. No parade-ground maneuver could save a regiment in such a predicament. There was only the luck of each man and the swiftness of foot. Each man must fall back on his own, firing if and when he had the opportunity. Regimental formation was sacrificed until reaching a position of safety, and the Michigan unit was thoroughly disorganized. But if the regiment was no longer recognizable because of its lack of a battle line, its regimental colors still indicated its presence. The colors—that pride of the regiment, that symbol of its identity, its fatiguing marches, its battle honors and losses, and its comradeship—still showed that the Wolverines had a fight in the Wheatfield. But the color guard was falling one by one as the regiment retraced its steps across the field, and at last the sole color bearer fell, grasping the staff in his agonies. Col. Harrison Jeffords, the commander of the dwindling regiment, saw the man fall and reacted immediately upon seeing a Confederate seize the flag from the hand of the suffering color bearer. Raising his drawn sword, the hatless Jeffords rushed after the Southerner, followed by several other officers and men of the regiment. Jeffords was first to reach the enemy around the newly captured prize and cut down the man with his sword, only to be attacked himself by several of the victim's vengeful comrades. A bayonet thrust through the chest of Colonel Jeffords brought him to his knees, and with the utmost difficulty soldiers of his command carried him off the field to prevent him from falling into enemy hands.

The hand-to-hand fighting that occurred in these last desperate moments of the battle in the Wheatfield signaled a drama that seldom occurred in the Civil War. The fight for the colors of the 4th Michigan epitomized the desperation of close combat. It was one of the few places where the bayonet was actually used as a killing tool, and Harrison Jeffords has become a part of history as the only regimental commander killed with the weapon during the war. But the futility of his death was soon matched by the futility of the Confederate invasion. General Lee's valiant men in gray would also be compelled to abandon the Wheatfield, and ultimately the battlefield. There was no harvest of wheat that summer in the Wheatfield. There was only a harvest of death.

KATHLEEN GOERG HARRISON has been a historian at Gettysburg National Military Park since 1976; she currently serves in that capacity and as cultural resources specialist. She is the author of *Nothing but Glory: Pickett's Division at Gettysburg*, as well as numerous articles on the battle.

Don't Give an Inch

July 2, 1863

B RIG. GEN. GOUVERNEUR KEMBLE WARREN STOOD TRANSFIXED BY THE
sight. The chief engineer of the Army of the Potomac had, moments
before, ascended the summit of Little Round Top to find no blue-clad
infantry in position. Only a few Signal Corps officers were there, and they
pointed out to him the line of III Corps troops to their front. Farther west,
toward the Emmitsburg Road, Warren could see woods that might hide Southern
troops. He sent a message to the 4th New York Battery posted above Devil's Den
to lob a shot over those woods. As the shell screeched overhead, anxious heads

turned to watch it; the gleam of musket barrels told Warren the horrible truth—the Southern lines overlapped the left of the III Corps.

Warren quickly sent aides to find infantry to occupy Little Round Top. Daniel E. Sickles, the III Corps commander, said he could spare no troops. However, Lieutenant Mackenzie soon met Major General Sykes, commanding the V Corps, which was then moving forward to support Sickles. Upon hearing Warren's message, Sykes told Mackenzie he would send a brigade from his 1st Division, led by Brig. Gen. James Barnes.

Sykes sent one of his staff officers back along the column to find Barnes. This officer encountered Col. Strong Vincent, commander of the division's 3rd Brigade. Only twenty-six, Vincent, colonel of the 83rd Pennsylvania, had been in command of the brigade since May 20. Vincent hailed the aide: "Captain, what are your orders?"

"Where is General Barnes?" replied Sykes's aide. "What are your orders?" Vincent repeated. "Give me your orders."

"General Sykes told me to direct General Barnes to send one of his brigades to occupy that hill yonder."

"I will take the responsibility of taking my brigade there," Vincent answered.

Without further hesitation, the young colonel, followed by brigade color bearer Oliver W. Norton, galloped back down the road toward Little Round Top. Finding the western slope too difficult to climb, the mounted men rode around to the hill's wooded eastern slope, then followed the trees to the southern end of the summit.

Because of the rocky terrain, Vincent dismounted to scout the area better. In his haste to explore the area, Vincent forgot his sword, which remained strapped to his horse. Soon, a Confederate artillery shell whistled overhead and struck nearby. The colonel realized that the brigade flag was the target. "Down with the flag, Norton!" he yelled. "Damn it, go behind the rocks with it!"

Vincent scouted the area by the time the four regiments of his brigade arrived. From right to left, Vincent placed the 16th Michigan, 44th New York, 83rd Pennsylvania, and 20th Maine. The brigade could muster scarcely 1,300 officers and men. The line occupied a spur twenty feet lower than the southern end of the crest of the hill. Here was the line Vincent defended.

Vincent's men were scarcely in position before a line of advancing Southern troops attacked the position. Three regiments of John B. Hood's division—4th Alabama and 4th and 5th Texas—emerged from woods at the base of the hill and charged forward, only to meet a sheet of flame from Union rifles. For over an hour, the Southerners tried unsuccessfully to push Vincent's men out of their strong position. Fighting spread to the Union left when two more Alabama regiments—the 15th and 47th—joined the fray. When Devil's Den fell to Confederate attacks, the 48th Alabama moved forward to assail Vincent's right.

Vincent was far from idle as the battle raged. He positioned himself on a rock behind his line so he could see what was happening. The colonel dispatched aides to find reinforcements and ammunition. Finally, however, a crisis threatened the line. The new Southern attack on his right began to overwhelm the

16th Michigan. Its right flank crumbled as soldiers headed for the rear, taking the regimental colors and Lt. Col. Norval Welch with them.

Vincent saw the regiment's trouble and ran to rally the men. "Don't give an inch," he called, brandishing his riding crop all the while. As he did, a bullet pierced his groin, creating a mortal wound. Even then help was arriving, because General Warren had not seen Vincent's brigade take position on the southern end of the hill. The general spied a column of troops marching toward the Peach Orchard and swiftly galloped down the hill to intercept the force, which was Brig. Gen. Stephen H. Weed's V Corps brigade. Warren detached Col. Patrick H. O'Rorke and the 140th New York to Little Round Top. O'Rorke's men crested the hill just as the 16th Michigan began to crumble. Their counterattack repelled the Alabamians and Texans and stabilized the line.

The mortally wounded Vincent died on July 7, just after his brigadier general's commission reached him.

Dr. Richard A. Sauers, a native of Lewisburg, Pennsylvania, received his MA and PhD in American history from the Pennsylvania State University. He is the author of numerous books, articles, introductions, and book reviews on various aspects of the Civil War, including *The Gettysburg Campaign, A Caspian Sea of Ink: The Meade-Sickles Controversy,* and *Advance the Colors! Pennsylvania Civil War Battleflags.*

Little Round Top

O N THE AFTERNOON OF THURSDAY, JULY 2, THE MEN OF THE FAMOUS Texas Brigade, now under the command of Brig. Gen. Jerome B. Robertson, heard the call to advance and with the other three brigades of John B. Hood's Confederate division stepped off on their mission. It was the hottest day of the week thus far, the haze in the overcast skies driving the temperatures into the low eighties. It was to be, perhaps, their best and worst day.

At about the center of the eighteen regiments from Alabama, Arkansas, Georgia, and Texas was the 5th Texas Infantry under the command of Col. R. M. Powell. For the most part, these were battle-hardened veterans who had taken a significant role in practically every major fight since the war began.

Had they begun the day eager to join the fight that had erupted the previous morning and gone so favorably for their side, this morning's events may have dampened their enthusiasm. Starting at sunrise, there had been much activity in the army around them, but little of it seemed to accomplish anything. By early afternoon, they had marched for more than an hour only to halt, wait, and start back from where they had come, starting all over again by way of another route.

Finally, after hours of starts and stops in marching column, the Texans formed for the planned attack on the Union left flank and crossed the Emmitsburg Road toward a thin line of woods beyond. Further on, the ground rose upward through a rocky field, which, by then, was topped by six guns of enemy artillery wreaking havoc with their approach.

Before they had moved more than a few hundred yards, the attack encountered even greater troubles. A gap opened in the center of Robertson's brigade, which then widened as the two parts moved forward at separate angles. Two Alabama regiments filled the gap, leaving the 4th and 5th Texas mingled among regiments of the wrong brigade. The rest of the Texas brigade, including its commander, moved in the other direction.

In time the other half of the brigade seized the rocky slope and the guns upon it, only to discover a valley and far more formidable hill beyond. Meanwhile, the 4th and 5th Texas pressed on, passing a formation of enormous boulders, which they later came to know as Devil's Den. The hill beyond it, toward which the Texans now moved, would become known as Little Round Top.

Encountering Union troops among the huge boulders, the two regiments to the Texan's left, the 44th and 48th Alabama, halted and engaged the enemy in the valley. As the 4th and 5th Texas climbed the rough slope, the 4th Alabama on their right dissolved among the rocks in the face of a withering fire and the fatigue of having marched nearly thirty miles that day.

Bearing the brunt of the frontal assault up a steep and rocky hill, the two Texas regiments struggled toward the enemy. They spent more than an hour between the base of the hill and a plateau just below the enemy line on the summit. Three times they mounted concerted efforts to reach the top but to no avail. With their colonel and lieutenant colonel down, darkness falling, and no progress in the face of a galling fire, they withdrew to safety behind Devil's Den.

When morning came again, the men of the 5th Texas assessed their loss and understood the damage that the short time on the rocky hill had inflicted on their once-robust regiment. Of the four hundred men who stepped across the Emmitsburg Road the day before, nearly two hundred were no longer in line. Thirty men of the 5th were dead, twenty more suffered mortal wounds, and more than ninety were on their way to Union hospitals or prisons.

More than a decade after the war, Gen. James Longstreet, the man who commanded both the Confederate attack on the second day and the more famous assault on the third, called the actions of his men on July 2 "the best three hours' fighting ever done by any troops on any battle-field." No regiment in Longstreet's assault fought harder, and none suffered greater casualties, than the 5th Texas Regiment.

Don Troiani's brushstrokes have captured the men of the 5th Texas at the climax of their ill-fated assault on Little Round Top. Desperately trying to climb the steep hill through boulders and brush while their commanders and comrades fell among them, the Texans pushed on despite the fire of a determined foe, reinforced by fresh infantry and a battery of artillery.

DR. THOMAS A. DESJARDIN has served as an archivist/historian at Gettysburg National Military Park and is the author of *Stand Firm Ye Boys from Maine: The 20th Maine and the Gettysburg Campaign*, a detailed description and analysis of the relationship between that famous regiment, commanded by Joshua Chamberlain, and their part in the fight for Little Round Top at Gettysburg.

Lions of the Round Top

F OR THE MEN OF THE 20TH MAINE, JULY 2, 1863, HAD OPENED WITH A march at daybreak to arrive on the Union right flank east of Wolf Hill. Here, Maj. Gen. George Sykes, commanding the V Army Corps, massed his troops to prepare for a projected attack on the enemy left. After General Meade's scouts reported unfavorable terrain, he abandoned an offensive and ordered the V Corps to cross Rock Creek and go into reserve.

Here the men remained until Southern artillery fired on the position of the III Army Corps. When Meade discovered the exposed position of the corps, he ordered Sykes to bring the V Corps to the left and hold the line at all costs. The corps began a rapid movement as soon as the orders were passed. In response to a request from an engineer officer for troops to occupy Little Round Top, the key to the Union left, Sykes detached a brigade from the 1st Division and sent it to seize the hill.

This brigade, led by Col. Strong Vincent of the 83rd Pennsylvania, quickly surmounted the hill and moved to the southern side of its crest. Here, along a spur halfway up the slope, Vincent deployed his four regiments to protect the Union left flank.

The 20th Maine, Col. Joshua Chamberlain commanding, was first in line. Vincent accompanied Chamberlain and pointed out his assigned position on the brigade's left. The Maine boys were to be the left of the entire Army of the Potomac. "You understand! Hold this ground at all costs!" Vincent emphasized to Chamberlain. Then he moved to the right to position his other regiments.

Chamberlain quickly deployed his men to take advantage of the large boulders and trees covering the slope. Raised in the summer of 1862, the 20th had yet to see any major fighting; even so, its strength this day was only 386 officers and men. Of these, almost one hundred had recently been assigned from the 2nd Maine, a two-year regiment that had just gone home for mustering out. The 20th was armed with Enfield rifled muskets, while the recent acquisitions still carried their Springfields.

As the 20th deployed, Chamberlain sent Company B to guard his left flank. The remaining nine companies were hardly in position when Southern troops of John B. Hood's division hit Vincent's right flank. The fighting slowly spread along the line toward the Maine troops. Suddenly, the Yankees could see gray-clad troops approaching their front. They proved to be Col. William C. Oates and his 15th Alabama, supported by the 47th Alabama on their left. These two regiments had climbed Big Round Top, stopped to rest, and then descended the slope to attack the Union left.

The Alabamians charged forward into a sheet of lead from Chamberlain's men. The Southern line "wavered like a man trying to walk into a strong wind," Oates wrote years later. Again and again the Alabamians came on, advancing and firing. Chamberlain wrote in his report that "the edge of the fight rolled backward and forward like a wave." The two lines slugged it out at close quarters, at times with hand-to-hand combat.

Unable to break the Union line, Oates sent some of his companies to flank the Maine unit's left. Chamberlain saw this maneuver, and, to counter it, he thinned his right companies to cover more ground, while Maj. Ellis Spear refused the left flank. This tactic rebuffed the next Confederate attack, although at a heavy cost. The attack bent the left wing back so much that the 20th's line probably resembled a horseshoe, the colors at the apex. Here, amid the carnage, Color Sgt. Andrew J. Tozier stood atop a boulder and protected the regiment's colors, an unmarked, thirty-four-star national flag made by the Philadelphia firm of Evans & Hassall.

The attackers had also suffered heavy casualties, and Colonel Oates was concerned about his men's ability to continue the assault. The 15th, like the rest of Evander Law's brigade, had moved into battle with little water, and this lack was beginning to tell. Oates could see bodies and blood everywhere; officers also reported Union troops to their flank and rear (some of Berdan's sharpshooters and Company B). Thus, Oates decided to retreat to Big Roundtop and re-form.

This was the state of affairs when momentous events happened within the ranks of the 20th Maine. Lt. Holman S. Melcher of Company F, the color company, sought permission to recover some of his wounded men from between the lines. Even as he asked Chamberlain, other officers also suggested a forward move. The colonel had decided to advance—a third of the regiment's men were dead or wounded and the rest were out of ammunition. Another attack would probably punch through the regiment and send it reeling back.

Chamberlain ordered his men to fix bayonets and charge. Then, with Melcher leading the color company, the entire regiment surged forward, catching the enemy completely by surprise. "My men went down upon the enemy with a wild shout," Chamberlain wrote. Oates had just ordered a withdrawal, and the Maine boys hastened the Alabamians' retreat. So confused was the initial melee that one Alabama officer fired his pistol at Chamberlain's head while offering his sword in surrender. As the 20th charged, Company B and the green-clad sharpshooters appeared in Oates's rear, causing further havoc. Oates later admitted that his men "ran like a herd of wild cattle" to escape the Union attack. Those who did not run quickly enough were seized as prisoners by pursuing Yankees. Oates's men finally stopped on Big Round Top; the 20th Maine, winded from its charge and long battle, halted in the valley between the hills. The 20th had suffered a loss of 125—29 killed, 91 wounded, 5 missing—32 percent of those engaged.

This painting shows, for the first time, the true appearance of the 20th Maine's national colors, hitherto unexamined by previous artists of this scene. The mix of Enfields and Springfields used by the regiment is also visible in this portrayal of the wild rush down the slope of Little Round Top, a far cry from earlier renditions involving the 20th Maine and 15th Alabama.

DR. RICHARD A. SAUERS, a native of Lewisburg, Pennsylvania, received his MA and PhD in American history from the Pennsylvania State University. He is the author of numerous books, articles, introductions, and book reviews on various aspects of the Civil War, including *The Gettysburg Campaign, A Caspian Sea of Ink: The Meade-Sickles Controversy,* and *Advance the Colors! Pennsylvania Civil War Battleflags.*

Barksdale's Charge

"I WISH YOU WOULD LET ME GO IN, GENERAL; I WOULD TAKE THAT battery in five minutes." It was now 6:00 P.M. on July 2. Brig. Gen. William Barksdale had become impatient as his brigade of Mississippians lay under Union artillery fire. Half of Lafayette McLaws's division was already engaged with Federals south of the Peach Orchard. The remaining two brigades were awaiting orders to advance.

Barksdale, a forty-one-year-old Mississippi politician, had compiled a solid combat record prior to Gettysburg. Always the officer to set an example, he called his four regimental commanders together for a conference before the attack. The general pointed to the high ground at the Peach Orchard and said, "The line before you must be broken . . . to do so let every officer and man animate his comrades by his personal presence in the front line."

Finally, McLaws sent orders for Barksdale to advance. The four Mississippi regiments (18th, 13th, 17th, and 21st, from left to right) climbed over a stone wall and dressed their lines as their general rode to the front and addressed the brigade. Then, when the order to advance was given, 1,500 voices raised the Rebel yell. Barksdale rode in front, waving his hat to encourage his troops. The brigade advanced quickly, easily driving back a Yankee skirmish line.

In the Peach Orchard, defending Union regiments saw Barksdale's men come forward toward them. Directly in the attack's path was Battery E, 1st Rhode Island Light Artillery, which had punished McLaws's men throughout the afternoon. Capt. George E. Randolph, artillery chief of the III Army Corps, saw the enemy infantry advancing. He quickly rode to the nearest infantry support, the 114th Pennsylvania. Randolph called to Capt. Edward R. Bowen to advance the 114th and save the artillery.

The 114th was a Zouave regiment from Philadelphia, uniformed in baggy red pants and red fezzes. The regiment arose and moved forward across the Emmitsburg Road to contest the Rebel attack. The Zouaves were supported on their left by the 68th Pennsylvania, while the 57th and 105th Pennsylvania regiments soon moved forward on their right. Under this cover, Battery E limbered up and withdrew, having suffered heavy losses in horses and men.

The 114th's alignment was broken as it climbed over the partially dismantled fences bordering the road. The regiment's right flank took cover at farmer John Sherfy's homestead. As the Mississippians entered effective rifle range, the Pennsylvanians opened a deadly fire. Confederate survivors later recalled that only the speed of their advance saved the brigade from heavier casualties.

Barksdale's men crashed into the Peach Orchard with an irresistible force. The 68th Pennsylvania soon retreated in confusion, leaving the 114th's left flank exposed. Meanwhile, the 13th and 17th Mississippi, led by Barksdale in person, attacked the Zouaves in front. For a time, the fighting was almost hand-to-hand. "Within a few feet of each other these brave men, Confederates and Federals, maintained a desperate conflict," wrote one Southern officer.

But the impetus of the charge remained with the Confederates. The 114th was slowly forced to yield ground, leaving a carpet of red-uniformed casualties behind. Surviving Zouaves retired to the northeast along the Emmitsburg Road, pursued by the Mississippians. As the 114th uncovered its front, the 73rd New York, held in reserve, fired into the oncoming Southerners. Unable to stop Barksdale's men, the New Yorkers soon joined the retreat.

"Forward, men, forward!" shouted Barksdale, alert to the tide of battle in favor of the South. As the 114th's position crumbled, the left flank unit—the 18th Mississippi—encountered the 57th Pennsylvania, positioned in and around the Sherfy farm. This Keystone unit, too, gave way before the Southern advance. A large number of 57th soldiers, ensconced in the Sherfy buildings for cover, were captured because the noise of battle made shouted orders impossible to hear.

Once the 57th retired, the 105th Pennsylvania, nicknamed the "Wild Cat Regiment," was attacked and also joined the retreat. Barksdale's three left regiments now joined in one line and swept the shaken Union line before it. The 21st Mississippi strayed to the right, attacking other Union units to the south. After driving these regiments away, the 21st advanced and eventually overwhelmed the 9th Massachusetts Battery at the Trostle House.

Barksdale's brigade then continued its advance, driving the Federal line north before turning east toward Cemetery Ridge. As darkness approached, Col. George L. Willard's Yankee brigade charged headlong into the Mississippians along Plum Run. After a brief fight, the disorganized Southern regiments fell back, leaving their gallant brigadier a mortally wounded prisoner. The entire brigade suffered a loss of 46 percent of its engaged strength. Its charge on the Peach Orchard had been one of the most magnificent charges of the war.

DR. RICHARD A. SAUERS, a native of Lewisburg, Pennsylvania, received his MA and PhD in American history from the Pennsylvania State University. He is the author of numerous books, articles, introductions, and book reviews on various aspects of the Civil War, including *The Gettysburg Campaign, A Caspian Sea of Ink: The Meade-Sickles Controversy*, and *Advance the Colors! Pennsylvania Civil War Battleflags*.

Retreat by Recoil

The 9th Massachusetts Battery

ON THE MORNING OF JULY 2, 1863, AS PART OF THE ARTILLERY RESERVE, Army of the Potomac, the 9th Massachusetts Battery was parked behind the Federal line, waiting for action. The unit had yet to see its first battle, having just joined the army from the Washington defenses.

When the battle opened on Gen. Daniel Sickles's front, reserve batteries moved to add strength to the defenders. Shortly after 4:00 P.M., the 9th began rolling toward the battle. Capt. John Bigelow led his six-gun battery forward. It halted briefly near the Abraham Trostle farm, then dashed forward to unlimber along the Wheatfield Road in rear of the Peach Orchard. Here, the battery joined a line of Yankee cannon pounding the advancing troops of James Longstreet's Confederate I Corps.

Unsupported by infantry, the 9th held its position until Brig. Gen. William Barksdale's Mississippi Brigade crashed into the Peach Orchard, breaking the infantry line and exposing the artillery to capture. Units withdrew until only the 9th was left. Brigade commander Lt. Col. Freeman McGilvery ordered Bigelow to get off the field before it was too late.

However, the captain was in a quandary. If his guns stopped firing, enemy skirmishers from Joseph Kershaw's brigade would close in, as would Barksdale's troops. Therefore, Bigelow ordered his men to "retire by prolonge." This meant that ropes were uncoiled from each cannon and tied to limbers, which then drew the guns off the field as the gunners continued to fire, the recoil from each blast pushing the smoothbore Napoleons backward.

Under a steady stream of fire from Kershaw's men, Bigelow's command retired over 400 yards across one of Trostle's pasture fields until the battery reached the corner of the field opposite the farm. Here, as the men limbered up and prepared to withdraw toward Cemetery Ridge, McGilvery appeared and shouted to Bigelow that there were no troops behind him. His battery was the only unit in front of a large gap toward which enemy troops were advancing. Bigelow must hold his position as long as possible to allow reinforcements to plug the gap!

Stone walls along each side of the field made retreat difficult, for there was only one gate into the farmhouse lane. Bigelow arrayed his six cannon in a semi-circle at the corner of the field. After sending the caissons to the rear, sweating artillerists emptied the limbers and placed rounds of ammunition on the ground by each gun for rapid fire. Soon, Kershaw's skirmishers appeared to the south, advancing slowly toward the battery. Lt. Richard S. Milton's section began firing canister at the approaching South Carolinians, keeping them at bay.

The commanders of the other two sections, Lts. Christopher Erickson and Alexander H. Whitaker, had their field of vision reduced by a small knoll that spread across the field to the west and southwest. Soon, however, the heads of an approaching line of battle could be seen. Both sections fired solid shot at what proved to be the 21st Mississippi, commanded by Col. Benjamin G. Humphreys. The men soon switched to canister, which broke the Southern line and caused the regiment to veer toward the left, in the direction of the Trostle farm.

The gunners soon switched to double charges of canister, with fuses cut so that the cans would explode near the muzzles of the fieldpieces. The heavy discharges of iron balls blew the gray-clad infantry back. Still, Southern rifle fire caused a heavy loss in men and horses. Recoil from the continued firing soon cramped the battery position, so Bigelow ordered Milton to take his section to the rear.

As Milton's two guns rolled rearward, the Rebels came on again. By this time, Erickson's section, on the left, was badly disabled. The lieutenant rode over to see if he could aid Whitaker's men. As he approached one of the cannon and asked if he could help, six bullets crashed into Erickson, killing him instantly. As he fell from his horse, Mississippians came into the battery and a hand-to-hand struggle ensued.

By this time, Bigelow realized that his men had to retreat. Bigelow himself was wounded when some of Kershaw's men fired a volley that the battery's bugler, Charles Reed, partially blocked with his horse. Chaos now abounded. "It is a wonder we were not all killed," recalled one of the cannoneers. Aided by Reed, the wounded Bigelow ordered his men to abandon the guns.

The remnant of the battery's men retreated toward Cemetery Ridge. They had held the Confederate attack over thirty minutes and allowed reinforcements to seal the breach. The cost was high. Of the sixty men remaining with guns, twenty-eight were killed, wounded, or captured. Eighty of the eighty-eight horses were slain. The battery had fired ninety-two of ninety-six canister rounds. Four guns were left on the field but retaken that night by XII Corps troops. The heroic stand of the 9th Massachusetts Battery was one of many such actions at Gettysburg.

DR. RICHARD A. SAUERS, a native of Lewisburg, Pennsylvania, received his MA and PhD in American history from the Pennsylvania State University. He is the author of numerous books, articles, introductions, and book reviews on various aspects of the Civil War, including *The Gettysburg Campaign, A Caspian Sea of Ink: The Meade-Sickles Controversy,* and *Advance the Colors! Pennsylvania Civil War Battleflags.*

The First Minnesota

July 2, 1863

THE MEN OF THE 1ST MINNESOTA WATCHED WITH INCREASING APPREHEN-
sion as the panorama unfolded before them. Solid veterans of a dozen
fights and two years of heavy campaigning, most of these transplanted
New Englanders had been toughened as recent pioneers to the new state of Minnesota. This was a regiment with a fine reputation, honed under regular army
colonels and noted for solid, reliable service. They had never deserted a post nor
turned their back on the enemy except under orders. Now their resolve would be
put to the ultimate test.

The 1st had arrived on the field early that morning after a hard two-week
march from Fredericksburg. They had been posted in reserve down near
Meade's headquarters, then shifted west to the ridge above Plum Run to support
the guns of Battery C, 4th U.S. Light Artillery. This was ground that Sickle's III
Corps should have held. But Sickle's advance and imminent collapse under pressure from Longstreet's assault on the Union left now put the entire Federal army
at risk.

The Minnesotans' Company L with their Sharps rifles was some distance
away supporting a battery. Company F was over near Little Round Top acting as
skirmishers, and Company C was still detached as division provost guard. Perhaps
262 men of the remaining eight companies stood in line just below the crest of
Cemetery Ridge. It was around 7:00 P.M. with the sun headed toward the hori-
zon as demoralized remnants of the III Corps streamed up the slope and past
the westerners. Two battle lines of Longstreet's corps, Alabamians of Wilcox's
brigade, appeared over the opposite crest barely 700 yards away. Rebel cannons
quickly went into battery and opened fire on the six guns just to the right of the
Minnesotans. The storm would soon be upon them.

II Corps commander Winfield Scott Hancock arrived at a gallop, found Col.
William Colvill, frontier lawyer, and asked, "Do you see those colors, Colonel?
We'll take them!" As his men strained with the intensity of the moment, Colvill
gave the commands: "Attention battalion! Right shoulder shift arms. Forward—
double quick—*march*!"

Professional soldiers now, the westerners obeyed as one. Each man knew
that their one chance of success, and survival, was to reach the broken ground
and boulders of Plum Run before more Rebels did. Men dropped at every step
as both artillery and the Alabama infantry concentrated their fire. Confederate
skirmishers advanced through the swale below as the 1st Minnesota moved from
double quick into a full run. Colvill yelled "charge," and the front rank dropped
their bayoneted muskets forward. But while the color guard and right wing swept
on, the left wing apparently twice received confusing orders to halt. As the color
moved away and their vulnerability in the open field became all too apparent,
they too rushed toward the creek.

Wilcox's 1,600 Alabamians were battle weary. Before Minnesota bayonets
reached them, the skirmishers ran back. The Minnesota thunderbolt smashed
into the Alabamians' first line of battle, and volleyed point-blank. That line,
already mixing with the second line as it crossed the stream, momentarily collapsed. In the broken ground of Plum Run confusion reigned supreme as three

lines of battle fought for control of the creek bed. It took only moments for Wilcox's men to reorganize and concentrate fire on the westerners, soon working around their flanks.

The Minnesotans felt bullets buzzing at them from three directions as their ranks thinned. They shifted toward the center and the color. Here Colonel Colvill fell, shot through the shoulder and thigh. Shouting to Captain Coates to "Take care of the boys," he rolled into the shelter of the creek bed. Over on the right, Lt. Col. Charles Adams was stuck five times as the Alabamians continued to move around the flank and toward the battery. Maj. Mark Downie and most of the officers of the left wing were shot as their flank was compromised. The national color, in tatters after a year of hard service and battle damage, went down three times until Corp. Henry O'Brien, last of the color guard, raised it again in the smoke-filled low ground of Plum Run.

Still holding the Rebels, but with the regiment nearly surrounded, someone ordered retreat. The men who gathered around the color feared the return almost more than holding their position. "We kited out of there," one boy remembered. Those able to do so ran a gauntlet of fire back up the slope past Confederates who had flanked them on both sides. Only forty-seven men—and the national color—made it.

As the Minnesotans fell exhausted along Cemetery Ridge, the end came for Wilcox's assault. Reinforcements rushed forward by Hancock bolstered Battery C on the right and helped push Confederates out of Plum Run on the left. Later, after dark and as scores of little firefights sounded gradually more distant, the survivors of the 1st Minnesota moved warily back down the slope to find their friends. Many of these lucky few would fall the next day and, like their comrades, rest forever at Gettysburg.

General Hancock remembered, "It was fortunate that I found there so grand a body of men as the First Minnesota. . . . The superb gallantry of those men saved our line from being broken. No soldiers, on any field, in this or any other country, ever displayed grander heroism."

STEPHEN E. OSMAN is the site manager of Historic Fort Snelling near Saint Paul, where the 1st Minnesota was organized and trained. A Civil War scholar since grade school, he is a fellow of the Company of Military Historians and frequently contributes to their journal. He has extensively researched early nineteenth-century military material culture and the role of Minnesota in the Civil War.

1st Minnesota Volunteer Infantry

T HE BATTLE OF GETTYSBURG WITNESSED COUNTLESS ACTS OF SACRIFICIAL gallantry. Soldiers of both armies mastered their fears and displayed almost superhuman bravery for ideals they cherished more than life itself. Gettysburg offered no more powerful example of this transcendent heroism than the charge of the 1st Minnesota Volunteer Infantry on the late afternoon and early evening of July 2, 1863.

Proud veterans of some of the war's bloodiest battles—First Bull Run, the Seven Days', and Antietam—the tough westerners had earned a matchless reputation as one of the finest outfits in Hancock's II Corps. Many men had fallen to bullets and disease since the 1st Minnesota departed Fort Snelling in the spring of 1861, and the unit numbered fewer than 400 men as they commenced the grueling march to Gettysburg. Their colonel, thirty-three-year-old William Colvill Jr., was a tall, barrel-chested former newspaper editor who had risen from a captaincy to regimental command. In the course of the march Colvill had suffered the ire of General Hancock's stern chief of staff, Col. Charles Morgan, for allowing some of his soldiers to cross the Monocacy River on logs and planks rather than splash across as instructed. At Morgan's order, brigade commander William Harrow had temporarily placed Colvill under arrest.

By the summer of 1863 Colvill and his men were used to such arbitrary acts of military martinetism. Is was part of what it meant to be a soldier, and no corps in the Army of the Potomac was more soldierly than that commanded by "Hancock the Superb."

By five o'clock on the afternoon of July 2, the tide of battle was rolling relentlessly toward Cemetery Ridge, the II Corps, and the 1st Minnesota. The advance and subsequent collapse of Sickles's III Corps—which had initially been in reserve, supporting batteries of artillery posted along the southern reaches of the low elevation—caused Hancock's troops to be fed piecemeal into the maelstrom to check Longstreet's juggernaut. Colvill's 1st Minnesota found itself occupying a position earlier held by Gen. John Caldwell's entire division. To make matters worse, two of the Minnesota companies had been detached, leaving only 262 men in line to meet the threat.

Though the Napoleon guns of Lt. Evan Thomas's Battery C, 4th U.S. Artillery, were blazing, Gen. H. R. Anderson's division was rolling steadily forward, shoving aside the remnants of the III Corps. "The stragglers came rushing through the lines," Minnesotan Alfred Carpenter noted, "whom we in vain tried to stop and at last gave it up entirely, believing they were more injury than help to us." On the Rebels came, Brig. Gen. Cadmus M. Wilcox's Alabamians in the vanguard, pushing across the brushy swale of a dry streambed and heading for the strategic crest of Cemetery Ridge.

As he did so often on that crisis-filled day, General Hancock took personal charge of the Federal defense. Accompanied by a single aide, the stalwart corps commander took in the situation at a glance. As he later confessed, "I saw that in some way five minutes must be gained or we were lost." Checking his horse alongside Colonel Colvill's line, Hancock exclaimed, "My God, are these all the men we have here? What regiment is this?"

"First Minnesota," Colvill responded.

Hancock pointed to the oncoming Confederate battle flags and snapped, "Advance, colonel, and take those colors!"

Colvill called his men to attention and ordered them forward. Muskets carried at right shoulder shift, with bayonets fixed, the slender line guided on the colors and started down the gentle slope at the double-quick. Alfred Carpenter remembered, "Comrade after comrade dropped from the ranks; but on the line went. No one took a second look at his fallen companion. We had no time to weep."

As the ever-thinning line neared the woody swale and the blazing Rebel ranks, Colvill—afoot and leading the advance in person—ordered his men to halt and fire. At a distance of thirty yards, the volley felled dozens of the enemy. Then Colvill shouted the command to charge. Down came the muskets of the front rank, flashing with steel, and the Minnesotans plowed into Wilcox's first line, hurling it back on those that followed. "I never saw cooler work done on either side," Colvill claimed, "and the destruction was awful."

As the deadly, close-range fight swirled through the brush and across the ravine, Colvill was twice wounded, and his second in command was hit six times. Capt. Nathan Messick was in command when the forty-seven survivors pulled back to their starting point, having bought Hancock and the Union those precious five minutes and then some—time paid for with the blood of more than two-thirds of those who made the charge.

BRIAN C. POHANKA has held editorial positions with several history magazines and was a senior researcher and writer on Time-Life Books' twenty-seven-volume history of the Civil War. A member of the Company of Military Historians, he serves in the ranks of the 5th New York Zouaves, a Civil War living history unit, and works to preserve the threatened legacy of Civil War sites.

Band of Brothers

July 3, 1863

As Gen. Robert E. Lee's Army of Northern Virginia swept north toward Pennsylvania in June 1863, it was joined by the 1st Maryland Battalion of seven companies, commanded by Lt. Col. James R. Herbert. These tough veterans had campaigned with Stonewall Jackson in the Valley and on the Peninsula, then had been detached from the army to guard the Shenandoah Valley. Now, as Lee's army headed toward Maryland, the men finally entered their native state for the first time during the war.

After fighting at Winchester, the 1st Maryland was assigned to Brig. Gen. Steuart's brigade of Johnson's division, of Ewell's II Corps. The brigade arrived on the Gettysburg battlefield late on July 1, after the firing had ended. Weather-beaten, with many soldiers barefoot, the battalion massed north of Culp's Hill and prepared to enter battle.

The battalion passed most of July 2 waiting for Ewell's attack. Once James Longstreet's I Corps opened the action on the Federal left, Ewell was to press the Union right flank and prevent reinforcements from reaching Longstreet's front. If the opportunity presented itself, Ewell was to launch a sustained attack.

Johnson's troops crossed Rock Creek late in the afternoon and surged forward up the steep slopes of Culp's Hill. The rugged terrain and Union skirmishers delayed the attack, and it was dark by the time the Southern troops approached Union breastworks erected earlier that day. By this time, most of the Union XII Army Corps had been withdrawn to reinforce the left, leaving a single brigade—George S. Greene's five New York regiments—on the crest of the hill. Greene's men repulsed several assaults on their position. Lt. Col. Herbert of the 1st Maryland fell severely wounded during one attack. Elsewhere, Southern troops found abandoned breastworks and occupied them in preparation for a further advance on July 3.

However, the XII Corps had returned after dark and was prepared to retake its position when morning dawned. Brig. Gen. Geary, commanding the corps' 2nd Division, placed his 1st and 2nd Brigades, commanded by Col. Candy and Brig. Gen. Kane, respectively, in position to the right and rear of Greene's men. Union artillery posted south of the Baltimore Pike supported the infantry.

Musketry fire began by 3:30 A.M. on July 3. Minutes later, Union artillery opened a fifteen-minute bombardment. Stunned by the sudden barrage, Johnson's infantry returned fire and charged the Union positions, only to be repulsed again and again. Geary had the luxury of reserve units that could replace his front line when the men exhausted their ammunition. In this way, the Union line remained fresh as regiments constantly replaced each other throughout the morning.

The Marylanders were not so fortunate. They fired off most of their ammunition within a short time and had to obtain a fresh supply to remain on the field. Maj. W. W. Goldsborough reported the plight of his command, and the men were soon resupplied.

Shortly after 10:00 A.M., Johnson sent Steuart's regiments, supported by Daniel's North Carolinians, to charge the Yankee line in a last attempt to crush the enemy. Steuart moved his troops to the left, then formed to assail Geary's men. No sooner had the brigade left its cover than Union riflemen opened a destructive fire on the charging column. One of the Union relieving regiments was the 1st Maryland Eastern Shore, and by chance brother literally met brother in combat.

An eyewitness described the Maryland Battalion's charge: "Nothing could surpass the regularity with which the Enemy advanced, their arms at a right shoulder shift, dressing as if upon parade to fill the vacancies in their diminishing ranks occasioned by the destructive fire which plowed into their solid columns. But being Right in front the men must have seemed to themselves in dressing to the Left to swerve from our fire. This probably caused the first wavering; their compact quick step was changed to a double quick, and that to a run; finally the foremost men rushed in as best they might upon us. Many continued to advance after receiving their death wounds, falling forward to expire within our lines."

A Federal soldier in the 1st Maryland Eastern Shore recalled the scene: "Clouds of dust raised by bullets striking the ground all around enveloped us, and, at times, shut out everything from sight. Leaves and twigs fell from the trees in showers. The intense heat, the nervous tension, the unmistakable odor of blood, together with the constrained position forced by loading and firing from the parapet induced nausea."

The charge by the two Confederate brigades failed. In the 1st Maryland, Maj. Goldsborough fell wounded. Of the battalion's 400 men, 56 were killed, 118 wounded, and 15 missing, a casualty rate of 47 percent. Found among the dead was a pet dog belonging to the battalion. When the brigade charged, the dog ran ahead of the Marylanders and actually entered the Union line. Gen. Kane saw the animal running on three legs after he was first wounded. "Regarding him as the only Christian minded being on either side, I ordered him to be honorably buried," wrote the general. For the gray-clad Marylanders, their sacrifice was written in blood on the slopes of Culp's Hill.

DR. RICHARD A. SAUERS, a native of Lewisburg, Pennsylvania, received his MA and PhD in American history from the Pennsylvania State University. He is the author of numerous books, articles, introductions, and book reviews on various aspects of the Civil War, including *The Gettysburg Campaign, A Caspian Sea of Ink: The Meade-Sickles Controversy,* and *Advance the Colors! Pennsylvania Civil War Battleflags.*

Newhall's Charge

DURING THE GREAT CAVALRY BATTLE AT GETTYSBURG JULY 3, 1863, Capt. Walter S. Newhall of the 3rd Pennsylvania Cavalry led a handful of troopers into the midst of the entire 13th Virginia Cavalry.

"McIntosh, as he saw the Confederate column advancing, sent his Adjutant-General, Captain Walter B. Newhall, with orders to Captains Treichel and Rogers, of the Third Pennsylvania Cavalry, whose squadrons were deployed as dismounted skirmishers on the enemy's right, to mount and rally their men for a charge on his flank as it passed. But sixteen men could get their horses, and with five officers they made for the battle-flag. Newhall, sharing the excitement of the moment, rushed in, by the side of Treichel and Rogers, at the head of the little band. Captain Miller, whose squadron of the Third Pennsylvania had been fighting mounted in skirmishing order, rallied it and fired a volley from the woods on the right as the Confederate column passed parallel with his line but a short distance off, and then, with sabres drawn, charged down into the overwhelming masses of the enemy" (*Pennsylvania Magazine of History and Biography* 35, no. 1 [1911]: 24).

Newhall was speared in the face by the Confederate flag bearer and unhorsed, but he survived the incident.

DON TROIANI

"Come On, You Wolverines!"

Geheorge Armstrong Custer's death on the Little Big Horn in 1876
has largely overshadowed the rest of his life. But Custer compiled a ster-
ling record as a cavalryman in the Civil War and made notable contri-
butions to the Gettysburg campaign, especially in a fight with Jeb Stuart's Rebel
cavalry on July 3.

Custer had seen plenty of fighting during the campaign. He took part in the
cavalry battles against Stuart's men on the edges of the Shenandoah Valley as
Lee moved north and the Union sought intelligence on the Southerners' inten-
tions. George Meade took command of the army on June 26, and three days later
Custer received promotion to brigadier general and command of a brigade of
Michigan regiments in Judson Kilpatrick's cavalry division. He was only twenty-
three, and the Union's youngest general.

He was nothing if not flamboyant. One of his cavalrymen, seeing his new commander for the first time, noted his "unique outfit," a suit of black velvet and gold lace, a crimson tie, shining buttons, and a black hat with a gold cord. "A keen eye would have been slow to detect in that rider with the flowing locks and gaudy tie, in his dress of velvet and of gold, the master spirit that he proved to be," he said. Custer's gaudy appearance notwithstanding, the officer later judged him to be "the most brilliant and successful cavalry officer of his time."

Custer and his men tangled with Stuart again in the Pennsylvania town of Hanover on June 30, and Custer's war nearly came to an end on July 2 during a cavalry skirmish at Hunterstown, north of Gettysburg. Leading a charge against Rebel horsemen under Wade Hampton, Custer had his horse shot out from under him and tumbled to the ground. He was saved by the quick thinking of one his troopers, who yanked Custer onto his saddle and rode off to safety.

On the afternoon of July 3, Stuart, with some 6,000 men in four brigades and some artillery, led his cavalry on a move around the Union army's right. Left unopposed, he could have severed the Baltimore Pike—the Army of the Potomac's main supply line—and attacked Meade from the rear even as Lee's infantry was assaulting Meade's front in the attack known as Pickett's Charge.

Stuart's men emerged from a patch of woods sometime around noon. In front stretched farmland and the buildings of the Rummel family. The approach to the pike seemed open. Stuart then had one of his batteries fire four shots, one in each direction of the compass, for reasons that have never been adequately explained. If he meant to flush out the Union cavalry, he succeeded.

Custer was about to rejoin Kilpatrick when David McMurtrie Gregg asked him to remain with his division to help deal with Stuart. "Custer, eager for the fray, had wheeled about and was soon on the field," recalled a Pennsylvania cavalryman.

Both sides launched attacks and counterattacks as the battle rolled across the farmlands. Custer contributed with some effective artillery fire and a largely ineffectual attack by the 5th Michigan. When the regiment was forced to retire, Custer placed himself in front of his 7th Michigan and raised his saber. "Come on, you Wolverines!" he shouted. "Custer led the charge half way across the plain, then turned to the left; but the gallant regiment swept on under its own leaders, riding down and capturing many prisoners," wrote one of his cavalrymen.

The battle ebbed and flowed, and Custer's Michigan regiments were forced to give way before the Rebels. Stuart sent in reinforcements from Wade Hampton's and Fitzhugh Lee's brigades. "A grander spectacle than their advance has rarely been beheld," wrote a Union horseman. "They marched with well-aligned fronts and steady reins. Their polished saber-blades dazzled in the sun."

Custer led another charge into the advancing Rebels, this time riding alongside the commander of the 1st Michigan. "Then it was steel to steel," wrote a participant. "For minutes—and for minutes that seemed like years—the gray column stood and staggered before the blow; then yielded and fled." Custer's horse was shot. Once again he found himself on foot in a hot place, but then he claimed a riderless mount and scrambled aboard.

Union attacks on the Confederate flanks persuaded Stuart that the time had come to retire. In the words of one historian, "It was Custer and the Wolverines who flew like bull dogs straight at the throat of the foes; who blocked his head-long charge; who pinned him to the ground while like wolves their comrade troops rushed upon his flanks." Stuart's attempt to attack the Union rear had failed.

TOM HUNTINGTON is the author of *Maine Roads to Gettysburg, Searching for George Gordon Meade: The Forgotten Victor of Gettysburg, Guide to Gettysburg Battlefield Monuments,* and *Pennsylvania Civil War Trails.* He lives in Camp Hill, Pennsylvania, about forty minutes from the Gettysburg battlefield.

Hampton's Duel

HE CAVALRY BATTLE EAST OF GETTYSBURG HAD BEEN RAGING FOR TWO hours on the hot afternoon of July 3, 1863. Jeb Stuart's horsemen had thus far been unable to drive their counterparts from the field. Both sides had fought both mounted and on foot, driving each other back and forth over the fields north of the Hanover Road.

For Brig. Gen. Wade Hampton, the day had not been good. The forty-five-year-old South Carolinian had been wounded in the head the day before by a Michigan trooper in the action at Hunterstown. His head still hurt, but Hampton was eager for battle. His brigade, massed under tree cover on Cress's Ridge, had watched the battle sway back and forth. When the 1st Virginia of Fitz Lee's brigade ran into trouble, Hampton sent two of his units—the 1st North Carolina and the Jeff Davis Legion—forward to assist the Virginians.

Quickly, though, Union reinforcements struck Hampton's two units, and they broke under the new attack. The general, realizing that his men had gone too far and were in serious danger, spurred his favorite charger, Butler, toward the broken ranks of his men.

Even as Hampton rode forward, Stuart ordered Hampton's brigade, supported by Fitz Lee's and John R. Chambliss's regiments, forward in a massed charge to win the victory. Hampton heard the noise of the advance, turned, and was surprised to see his brigade moving forward.

Yankee cavalrymen who saw the massed horsemen in gray start their advance were awed at the sight. "A grander spectacle than their advance has rarely been beheld," wrote Capt. William E. Miller of the 3rd Pennsylvania Cavalry. "They marched with well-aligned fronts and steady reins. Their polished blades dazzled in the sun."

Union artillery soon opened gaps in the line, but still the Rebels came. Brig. Gen. David M. Gregg, commanding the Union cavalry, gathered up units to oppose the oncoming Southerners. George Custer placed himself at the head of the 1st Michigan and charged the surging mass head-on. As the opposing forces crashed into each other, Union troopers from Michigan and Pennsylvania units attacked the right flank, while New Jersey and Pennsylvania companies charged headlong into the Confederate left. The entire field became a frenzied mass of confusion.

One of these Yankee charges, led by troopers from the 1st New Jersey Cavalry, penetrated the Southern host and encountered General Hampton. The six-foot Hampton was surrounded by enemy troopers as he fought for his life. The general downed two opponents with his keen sword arm, then fired his pistol at another group of assailants.

Just then, two comrades, Privates Moore and Dunlap of the Jeff Davis Legion, spurred forward to aid their commander. The two privates helped drive off some blue-clad troopers, but both went down in a renewed attack.

By this time, Hampton had been pressed back to a fence in his rear as more Union troopers reached him. The general shot a third, then was badly wounded in the head when a New Jerseyan thrust under Hampton's parry and reopened the July 2 wound. In his return thrust, Hampton's strong arm cut through the hapless Yankee's head, killing him.

Sgt. Nat Price of the 1st North Carolina and Private Jackson of Cobb's Legion now saw Hampton's predicament and came to his aid. Sergeant Price shot down an opposing trooper who was aiming a blow at the general's head. Throwing himself between the wounded Hampton and the Federals, Price shouted, "General, general, they are too many for us; for God's sake leap your horse over the fence; I'll die before they shall have you."

Injured and half blinded by blood flowing from his head wounds, Hampton obeyed the sergeant's urgent request. He spurred Butler over the fence, but just as horse and rider were in midair, a bullet struck Hampton in the right hip. Hampton remained mounted and headed toward the rear, turning brigade commander over to Col. Lawrence S. Baker of the 1st North Carolina.

DR. RICHARD A. SAUERS, a native of Lewisburg, Pennsylvania, received his MA and PhD in American history from the Pennsylvania State University. He is the author of numerous books, articles, introductions, and book reviews on various aspects of the Civil War, including *The Gettysburg Campaign, A Caspian Sea of Ink: The Meade-Sickles Controversy*, and *Advance the Colors! Pennsylvania Civil War Battleflags*.

The Civilians of Gettysburg

W HEN PEOPLE THINK OF THE GETTYSBURG BATTLEFIELD, THEY PICTURE the fields, hills, and woods of the National Military Park. Many do not realize that the town itself became part of the battlefield, with its citizens unwilling and powerless observers to war.

In 1863, Gettysburg—the seat of Adams County—had a population of about 2,400. Both the Lutheran Theological Seminary and Pennsylvania College (later Gettysburg College) called it home. The population was largely white, but African Americans made up about 8 percent. Many black citizens wisely fled the area as the Confederates approached Pennsylvania. The Rebels had been sweeping up African Americans and sending them back South into bondage, not caring whether they were escaped slaves or free American citizens.

Gettysburg received a taste of war on June 26, when Rebels under Jubal Early arrived. Early demanded food, hats, and shoes or—if that was not possible—$10,000. Gettysburg could not comply, and Early departed for York before he could press his demands. The town heaved a collective sigh of relief, but much worse was to come.

The arrival of John Buford and his Union cavalry on June 30 presaged the coming storm. Fighting erupted the next morning. That afternoon, Union troops of the XI Corps marched through town, and officers advised civilians to take shelter. As Maj. Gen. Oliver O. Howard rode through streets largely empty of citizens, he was struck by the sight of a young woman standing on her porch and waving a handkerchief to encourage the Union soldiers. It wasn't long, though, before those soldiers were retreating through town, the victorious Rebels at their heels.

The Federals who had not been killed or captured moved south to Cemetery Hill, leaving Gettysburg occupied by the Rebels. John Rupp, a tanner who lived on Baltimore Street, found himself between the lines. He hid in his cellar while Union soldiers occupied his front porch and fired through the house at Confederate soldiers in the back. Afterward, Rupp said, he collected a double handful of spent minié balls from his house.

Further north on Baltimore Street, Rebel sharpshooters occupied the upstairs of the McCreary family's house. "We did not dare to look out of the windows on the Baltimore side of the street [because] sharpshooters from Cemetery Hill were watching all the homes for Confederate sharpshooters and picking off every person they saw," recalled Albertus McCreary. One of the Rebels they picked off was Corp. William Poole, shot as he sheltered behind an overturned table at the McCreary's.

Mary McAllister, who lived on Chambersburg Street, helped Union wounded at Christ Lutheran Church. "Every pew was full," she said, "some sitting, some lying, some leaning on others. They cut off legs and arms and threw them out the windows."

Thomas Carson was a clerk at the Gettysburg Bank, just down York Street from the central square, also known as the Diamond. When a spent shell crashed through his attic widow and landed in the front hall, the Carsons decided to take shelter in the bank vault. His wife's brother, Charles O. Hunt, was a lieutenant in the 5th Maine Battery. When Hunt was wounded near the seminary on July 1, he received permission to recover at his sister's in town. When he arrived, he found nineteen people and two dogs sheltering in the bank vault. On July 3 Hunt and the rest of the town's inhabitants endured the cannonade that preceded Pickett's Charge, the terrible thunder shaking buildings to the foundations.

Not everyone in town fled or hid. John Burns was nearly seventy years old and somewhat eccentric when the Rebels arrived on July 1. He grabbed his musket and fought with the Union soldiers of the Iron Brigade. Burns was wounded three times during the fighting but lived to enjoy his fame as "the old hero of Gettysburg."

Amazingly, only one Gettysburg citizen—Mary Virginia "Jennie" Wade—was killed during the battle. Her sister, Georgia Wade McClellan, had given birth on June 26, and Jennie was tending to her at Georgia's house on Baltimore Street near Cemetery Hill. On July 3 a bullet, probably fired by a Confederate sharpshooter, passed through one door and an open doorway before hitting Jennie in the back and killing her as she baked bread.

The contending armies moved on after the battle, leaving hellish scenes of death and destruction behind them. Public buildings and churches now served as hospitals, crammed with the wounded. "The atmosphere is loaded with the horrid smell of decaying horses and the remains of slaughtered animals, and it is said, from the bodies of men imperfectly buried," wrote a Gettysburg woman. "I fear we shall be visited with pestilence, for every breath we draw is made ugly by the stench."

The battle had ended for Gettysburg. The task of recovery still lay ahead.

TOM HUNTINGTON is the author of *Maine Roads to Gettysburg, Searching for George Gordon Meade: The Forgotten Victor of Gettysburg, Guide to Gettysburg Battlefield Monuments,* and *Pennsylvania Civil War Trails.* He lives in Camp Hill, Pennsylvania, about forty minutes from the Gettysburg battlefield.

The Emmitsburg Road

O N THE AFTERNOON OF JULY 3, 1863, THE THIRD AND FINAL DAY OF THE battle of Gettysburg, Confederate Gen. Robert E. Lee ordered a grand charge across a mile of open ground to break the center of the Union line stretching south along Cemetery Ridge.

The assaulting column had about 13,000 men, with the three Virginia brigades of Maj. Gen. George Pickett's division forming the right wing of the attack. The front line of the left wing consisted of the four brigades of Maj. Gen. Henry Heth's division (commanded by Brig. Gen. James Johnston Pettigrew after Heth was wounded on July 1). The four brigades were Fry's Tennessee and Alabama brigade; Pettigrew's North Carolina brigade (including the 11th, 47th, 26th, and 52nd Regiment North Carolina Troops), commanded by the 52nd's Colonel Marshall; Davis's Mississippi brigade (with one North Carolina regiment, the 55th); and Brockenbrough's Virginia brigade. Behind Pettigrew were two North Carolina brigades of the wounded W. Dorsey Pender's division, placed under the command of sixty-two-year-old Maj. Gen. Isaac R. Trimble shortly before the charge: Scales's brigade (including the 38th, 13th, 34th, 22nd, and 16th Regiments North Carolina Troops), commanded by the 34th's Colonel Lowrance after Scales was wounded on July 1, and Lane's brigade (including the 7th, 37th, 28th, 18th, and 33rd Regiments North Carolina Troops). Unlike Pickett's fresh troops, almost all of Pettigrew's and Trimble's units had fought and suffered severe losses on the battle's first day.

This assault, doubtless the most famous in American history, is known as Pickett's Charge, a name that fails to acknowledge the role of more than half of the men in the attack. The North Carolinians' participation has never been fully acknowledged and has been ignored by the likes of Ken Burns and Shelby Foote.

Don Troiani's dramatic painting helps fill this historic gap, depicting the moment Trimble and his two North Carolina brigades, having just advanced across a mile of open ground under heavy artillery fire, attempt to cross the Emmitsburg Road, some 200 yards in front of Brig. Gen. Alexander Hay's troops of the 3rd Division, II Corps, Army of the Potomac, lining the stone wall on Cemetery Ridge. Ahead of Trimble, soldiers with the flag of the 52nd Regiment North Carolina Troops are shot down as they scale the Emmitsburg Road's eastern fence. Trimble rides at the flag of the 7th Regiment North Carolina Troops as the men of the 7th, commanded by Maj. J. McLeod Turner, enter the road after first knocking down its western fence. Someone close by calls out, "Three cheers for the Old North State," and General Trimble, astride his mare, Jinny, turns to his aide, Charles Grogan, and says: "Charley, I believe those fine fellows are going into the enemy's line." Trimble is mistaken. "As soon as the Confeds. began to climb the hither fence the men opened fire upon them," recalled Chaplain Stevens of the 14th Connecticut, "and the result was a dreadfully bloody one." Intense blasts of musketry pour down from the Union forces along Cemetery Ridge, repelling the Confederate attack. One sixteen-foot rail of the fence is drilled by 836 shots.

To the upper left is Bryan's farm, and ahead is the tall elm tree used by Trimble as his point of direction during the charge. The men of Lane's brigade carry Austrian Lorenz and Richmond Rifle muskets and other arms in mixed quantities. English observer Arthur Fremantle described the uniforms of these soldiers: "There is the usual utter absence of uniformity as to colour and shape of their garments and hats: grey of all shades, and brown clothing, with felt hats, predominate."

Who could have foreseen that the outcome of the decisive battle of the war would hang momentarily on a stout Pennsylvania post-and-rail fence? "Had there been no fence in the way in the third day's fight at Gettysburg I think Scales', Lane's and Pettigrew's brigades would have driven the Federals from their line," concluded Henry C. Moore, acting adjutant of the 38th Regiment North Carolina Troops.

Even though repulsed, the North Carolinians took satisfaction in the message Trimble sent to Lane after the charge: "General Trimble . . . directs me to say that if the troops he had the honor to command today for the first time couldn't take that position, all hell can't take it." Richmond County's Capt. B. F. Little of the 52nd put it another way, "The only 'giving way' that I could see on the part of Pettigrew's Brigade was the 'giving way' by falling to the earth, killed or wounded."

(The flags of the 7th and 52nd Regiment North Carolina Troops, captured July 3, 1863, are in the North Carolina Museum of History in Raleigh.)

MICHAEL W. TAYLOR, PhD, a lawyer and Vietnam veteran, has written about the North Carolina troops in the Pickett-Pettigrew-Trimble charge in *Gettysburg Magazine* and is the author of *The Cry Is War, War, War* and *To Drive the Enemy from Southern Soil.*

Toward the Angle

B Y THE TIME HE RODE ONTO THE DEADLY FIELDS ALONG THE EMMITSBURG
Pike on July 3, 1863, Gen. Richard Brooke Garnett, Confederate States
Army, had seen service across the North American continent. The Virginian had gained entry to West Point through family connections but did not
perform there with much academic distinction. For two decades after graduating
from the military academy, Dick Garnett marched across the country as a subaltern with the 6th United States Infantry. In 1854, Garnett left Fort Laramie just
before his replacement, Lt. John Grattan, became famous by being massacred.
Garnett later served in Bleeding Kansas, then led troops through Utah's "Mormon War" and on across the Sierra Nevada to California.

Dick Garnett's Civil War began on Virginia's Peninsula under Georgian
Thomas R. R. Cobb. He then ran afoul of the inflexible Stonewall Jackson while
commanding that famous soldier's old brigade at the battle of Kernstown in
March 1862. Court martial proceedings dragged on for months then faded
away. General R. E. Lee eventually transferred Garnett away from Jackson, thus
salvaging the junior officer's career. By September 1862, Brig. Gen. Garnett

held command of the brigade that had been Gen. George E. Pickett's and still belonged to Pickett's division.

Garnett led his brigade of five Virginia regiments (8th, 18th, 19th, 28th, and 56th Infantry) with marked bravery but little luck. The colonel of the 8th Virginia described Garnett as "not a man of much mental force [but] one of the noblest and bravest men I ever knew."

As the Army of Northern Virginia marched toward its date with destiny at Gettysburg, Garnett found further bad fortune. A staff officer's fractious horse "slashed out" and kicked the general's ankle. Writing from Chambersburg to a lady friend, Dick Garnett complained on June 25, 1863, that his damaged leg remained "quite sore," making him doubtful that he could ride for another week.

Early on the afternoon of July 3, Garnett discovered that he could ride well enough to lead his brigade in a desperate undertaking. Astride a bay mare, the general rode out at the head of the left element of Pickett's front line in what would become the most famous attack in American military history. One of Garnett's Virginians, who had been on skirmish duty beyond the ridge near the jump-off point, saw "a glittering forest of bright bayonets" as the brigade came out from cover to begin the advance "with steady step and superb alignment." "The rustle of thousands of feet amid the stubble" stirred up "a cloud of dust, like the dash of spray at the prow of a vessel." A torrent of gunfire soon banished the spectacle's spell, a participant wrote, as "thousands of deadly missiles rac[ed] through the air to thin our ranks."

One hostile round hit Garnett's mare and killed her outright. He switched to his best horse, a spirited bay gelding, and continued forward. Soldiers marveled at their "cool, gallant, noble brigade commander," riding high above the infantry through the sleeting metal that raged about them. "Steady, men! Steady!" he yelled above the roar. "Don't double-quick. Save your wind and your ammunition for the final charge." As the Virginians surged toward their enemies' front line at the famous stone fence, the air filled with a noise "like the blast through the top of a dry cedar or the whirring sounds made by the sudden flight of a flock of quail. It was . . . canister." Within a few yards of the stone fence the torrent of fire knocked Dick Garnett to the ground, dead on the spot, surrounded by hundreds of his dead or wounded soldiers. The gelding also fell mortally wounded.

Brig. Gen. Richard Garnett's body disappeared in the carnage left behind by the charge, even though antebellum friends in Union service searched for it. One of Garnett's colonels reported details of the death of both general and horse (his estate received $675 for the loss of the mount), but his corpse went unidentified into a quiet grave. Decades later, a comrade recognized Garnett's sword for sale in a Baltimore pawn shop. The sword eventually reached the family, but Garnett's burial place will remain forever unknown. He probably rests in the great mass grave of Confederate dead from Gettysburg in Hollywood Cemetery, Richmond. No Confederate general suffered a demise more dramatic than Garnett's, nor a postmortem fate more mysterious.

ROBERT K. KRICK is the author of numerous articles about the Civil War, including *Stonewall Jackson at Cedar Mountain,* which won the Douglas Southall Freeman Prize for Best Book in Southern History, and *Stonewall Jackson and Other Confederates: Chapters on the Army of Northern Virginia,* which includes an essay on General Garnett's problems with Jackson.

Rock of Erin

July 3, 1863

A PART OF THE FAMED PHILADELPHIA BRIGADE, THE 69TH PENNSYLVANIA had been recruited from the Irish population of the city in the summer of 1861. Assigned to the II Army Corps, the regiment had participated in most campaigns of the Army of the Potomac. Now, hard campaigning had reduced the thousand men of the original regiment to a mere 258 officers and men. The regiment's tattered colors included a state-issued national flag and a green flag containing the state coat of arms and three Irish symbols—the wolfhound, round tower, and sunburst.

Upon arrival on the battlefield early on the morning of July 2, the brigade occupied the center of the Union line on Cemetery Ridge. The 69th deployed in front of the now-famous Copse of Trees. During the fighting that afternoon, the regiment suffered twenty-eight casualties and helped rescue Battery B, 1st Rhode Island, which had been threatened by advancing Georgia troops.

The morning of July 3 dawned hot and humid. Skirmishing continued along the lines of battle, but the men of the 69th occupied themselves with trying to keep cool. Soldiers erected makeshift shelters by fixing bayonets, stabbing the muskets into the ground, and stretching rubber blankets and tents across the muskets to bring some relief from the heat.

And then, at one o'clock, Confederate artillery pieces opened fire on Cemetery Ridge. A storm of shot and shell descended on the center of the Union line as Southern artillerists paved the way for the great infantry assault to follow. A veteran of the 69th recalled that the cannon fire was not very deadly to the infantry line, but because of the number of flying missiles, the men hugged the ground, knowing that at any moment they could be "ploughed into shreds."

As Pickett's division emerged from the woods on Seminary Ridge and began its steady advance toward the Union line, their relentless, onward tramp elicited admiration from Union soldiers watching the grand spectacle. "No holiday display seemed more imposing, nor troops on parade more regular," wrote Pvt. Anthony W. McDermott.

As the Southerners came forward, Col. Dennis O'Kane ordered his men to arise from their scant cover behind a stone wall and get ready to meet the enemy. Reminding his men that they were defending the sacred soil of the Keystone State, O'Kane ordered the regiment to refrain from opening fire "until they came so close to us, that we could distinguish the whites of their eyes." Brig. Gen. Alexander S. Webb, commanding the brigade, also exhorted the regiment to do its duty.

As the enemy approached, two guns of Lt. Alonzo Cushing's Battery A, 4th United States, were run down to the stone wall on Company I's front. Their fire heartened the infantry but also inadvertently killed some of Company I's men before they could get clear of the field of fire. On the regiment's left rear, Capt. Andrew Cowan unlimbered his 1st New York Battery and opened on the approaching Confederates.

Still, the enemy came on. All order was lost as Pickett's men reached the Emmitsburg Road, some 250 yards in front of the Yankee line. As the range decreased, members of the 69th opened fire on the mass of men in butternut and gray climbing over the stout wooden fences bordering the road. Most, however, obeyed O'Kane's order and waited.

Then, the mass of gray surged forward, all brigade and regimental order lost as units became intermingled in one mass. In front of the 69th, Brig. Gen. Richard B. Garnett's Virginians came on, closing to within fifty yards of the stone wall before Colonel O'Kane ordered his men to fire. That morning, most members of the 69th had gathered up the muskets of fallen Union and Confederate soldiers from the previous day's fighting and collected them along the wall, loading as many weapons as could be made serviceable. Many were smoothbores loaded with buck and ball ammunition.

Thus, when the 69th opened fire at short range, the effect was deadly. "The slaughter was terrible," recalled Corp. John Buckley. The 69th's fire caused a momentary halt in front of its line, but troops from Garnett's and Brig. Gen. Lewis Armistead's brigades rushed forward across the wall to the 69th's right, forcing back the 71st Pennsylvania and threatening the 69th. To counter the threat, the three right companies—Companies A, I, and F—changed front to meet the attack.

At the same time, troops to the left abandoned the stone wall, and Confederates surged across, forcing back Companies G, K, and B. Hammered into a rough crescent, the 69th stood its ground and fought on. Soldiers in blue and gray were so close together that when they struck at each other with rifle butts, "they could not inflict any disabling injury," wrote McDermott. The hand-to-hand combat was deadly. Joseph McKeever recalled that "everybody was loading and firing as fast as they could." The mass of Confederates did likewise, and McKeever, years later, wondered how the 69th survived.

Quickly, the tide turned as reinforcements moved in toward the Bloody Angle to hem in the Southerners and force surrender or retreat. Armistead went down with a mortal wound, and the crossfire from the 69th and troops moving up proved decisive. The remnant of the 69th was suddenly overwhelmed with hundreds of prisoners, as many enemy soldiers surrendered rather than take their chances running back across the fields to the rear. Battle flags were seized as trophies by advancing troops; strangely enough, no soldier in the 69th was credited with any such captures.

For the 69th Pennsylvania, the cost was high—32 killed, 71wounded, and 18 taken prisoner—121 of the 256 in line that afternoon. Colonel O'Kane was mortally wounded and died on July 5; Lt. Col. Martin Tschudy was slain; and Maj. James Duffy, seen here in the painting, was shot through the thigh and eventually succumbed to the injury six years later. The regiment had covered itself in glory and had performed a heroic act by remaining in position and helping blunt the force of Pickett's Charge.

DR. RICHARD A. SAUERS, a native of Lewisburg, Pennsylvania, received his MA and PhD in American history from the Pennsylvania State University. He is the author of numerous books, articles, introductions, and book reviews on various aspects of the Civil War, including *The Gettysburg Campaign, A Caspian Sea of Ink: The Meade-Sickles Controversy,* and *Advance the Colors! Pennsylvania Civil War Battleflags.*

The High-Water Mark

July 3, 1863

T HE BOMBARDMENT WAS FINALLY OVER. FOR OVER AN HOUR AND A HALF, the Virginians of Maj. Gen. George E. Pickett's division had lain under Federal artillery fire that overshot the line of Southern cannon to their front. Scores of men had been killed and mangled, but now the time had come for the infantry assault on the center of the Army of the Potomac.

Pickett formed his division in two lines. Brig. Gens. Richard B. Garnett and James L. Kemper placed their troops in the first line. Following behind in support was Brig. Gen. Lewis A. Armistead's brigade. Armistead, forty-six years old, had been born in North Carolina but moved to Virginia at an early age. He had attended West Point but was dismissed after cracking a mess plate over classmate Jubal Early's head during an argument. Later, Armistead was commissioned directly into the Regular Army and performed gallantly during the Mexican War. Now, he was leading his men forward to attack troops under the command of one of his closest friends, Winfield Scott Hancock.

While the brigade's five regiments formed in line, Armistead walked up and down the line, encouraging his men to do their duty. Turning to the color bearer of the 53rd Virginia, the general asked, "Sergeant, are you going to put those colors on the enemy works over yonder?"

"If mortal man can it shall be done, sir," was the brief reply.

The division then advanced. Armistead's regiments, from left to right, were the 38th, 57th, 53rd, 9th, and 14th Virginia. The general himself marched on foot in front of his men. Lt. John H. Lewis recalled Armistead: "With his hat on his sword he led his brigade, being in front of it, and cheering it on. His men saw him. They saw his example. They caught his fire and determination, and then and there they resolved to follow that heroic leader until the enemy's bullets stopped them."

Shot and shell crashed into Pickett's ordered ranks as the gray line steadily marched over the fields toward Cemetery Ridge. The veteran soldiers quickly filled gaps caused by artillery projectiles. As the division neared the position of Hancock's troops, musketry fire was added to the artillery, which now switched to canister. Garnett's and Kemper's brigades dissolved into mobs of men but still pushed up to the stone wall marking the Yankee position.

By the time Armistead's brigade reached the area in front of the Angle, a Confederate officer wrote later, the survivors were "a mingled mass from fifteen to thirty deep." Casualties were high. Directly in front lay the remnant of Battery A, 4th United States Artillery, commanded by Lt. Alonzo H. Cushing. The battery comprised six 3-inch ordnance rifles, but the bombardment had shattered the unit and left few men to service the pieces. Cushing himself was shot dead as his last canister rounds were fired point-blank into Garnett's men.

Armistead realized the futility of exchanging fire with the defenders, so he charged forward, shouting, "Come on boys! Give them the cold steel! Who will follow me?"

At least 150 Virginians leaped over the wall, driving away the 71st Pennsylvania and capturing some of Cushing's cannon. By this time, the flag of the 53rd Virginia had gone down ten times; the most recent color bearer was shot as he surmounted the stone wall. When the flag fell, Lt. Hutchings Carter picked it up and urged his men on. The colors of the 14th and 57th Virginia also followed the general.

Other Confederates following Armistead turned aside and engaged the 69th Pennsylvania in hand-to-hand combat along the wall. This predominantly Irish regiment was positioned directly in front of the clump of trees. When the 71st fell back, the 69th refused its right and maintained its position. Southern units to the north of the Angle reached the wall and engaged Hancock's 3rd Division.

Now was the critical moment of the attack—reinforcements might enable the advance to continue.

Armistead pushed forward toward more of Cushing's guns. Just as he was about to place a hand on the barrel of the nearest piece, the 72nd Pennsylvania, located behind Cushing's guns, fired a deadly volley that mortally wounded Armistead and brought the Southern advance to a sudden halt. Brig. Gen. Alexander S. Webb, commanding the Philadelphia Brigade, tried to get the 72nd to charge, to no avail. The men preferred to fire into the mass of enemy soldiers in their front.

But more reinforcements arrived from the left, and those Confederates who had not become casualties had to retreat. All three flags that followed Armistead were captured; all three had been planted next to the same artillery piece. Armistead, mortally wounded, gave the Masonic sign for distress and was rescued by members of the 72nd Pennsylvania. He was carried back to a field hospital and died on July 5. His brigade had suffered 63 percent casualties and had earned the honor of fighting at the high-water mark of the Confederacy.

Dr. Richard A. Sauers, a native of Lewisburg, Pennsylvania, received his MA and PhD in American history from the Pennsylvania State University. He is the author of numerous books, articles, introductions, and book reviews on various aspects of the Civil War, including *The Gettysburg Campaign, A Caspian Sea of Ink: The Meade-Sickles Controversy,* and *Advance the Colors! Pennsylvania Civil War Battleflags.*

"Give Them Cold Steel, Boys"

CEMETERY RIDGE, SOUTHEAST OF GETTYSBURG, PENNSYLVANIA, JULY 3, 1863. Give or take a few minutes, it is 3:30 P.M.; the heat is oppressive, the humidity stifling, the lingering smoke acrid. For the Virginians of Pickett's division deadlocked in a firefight with the 69th and 72nd Pennsylvania regiments, holding a portion of the stone wall and the crest, respectively, the critical moment has arrived. While the battered wedges of Pettigrew's and Trimble's

regiments on their left edge forward against the maelstrom of musketry emitting from Hays's division holding the crest, the reticent remnants of Garnett's brigade and the left regiments of Kemper's brigade cling tenaciously to the portion of the stone wall they had seized only moments before from the 71st and the right companies of the 69th Pennsylvania regiment. But now they are leaderless. Pickett is too far to the rear, vainly seeking supports to buoy his crumbling, enveloped right flank; Kemper has fallen, grievously wounded; Garnett's lifeless body lays pinned beneath an aide's mangled horse; few field and line officers remain unscathed. Pushing through the mingling mass, Brig. Gen. Lewis A. Armistead, afoot, presses forward with his five regiments.

Armistead quickly surveys the desperate situation; the Union line ahead must be broken. Turning to the commander of his center and guiding regiment, Lt. Col. Rawley W. Martin, Armistead calls, "Martin, we can't stay here; we must go over that wall." Martin responds, "Then we'll go forward," and seeks his colors. The colors of his 53rd Virginia have fallen several times since Sergeant Blackburn had pledged to plant them on the enemy works "if mortal man can do it." After others had fallen, Robert Tyler Jones, despite a painful arm wound, had brought the flag to the wall, but now a head wound incapacitates him. As Martin cries, "Forward the colors!" Lt. Hutchings L. Carter takes them from Jones and scales the wall with Martin. Armistead turns to the milling hoard, reaffixes his hat on his sword tip, and hollers, "Who will follow me?" Then swinging his sword toward the crest, Armistead commands, "Give them cold steel, boys!" and leaps forward past one of the now-silent Ordnance Rifles Cushing's men had rolled to the wall.

It had taken Armistead and his men just over twenty minutes to reach this point. Pickett had arranged his division in two lines. The front line consisted of two brigades: Kemper's on the right (from right to left, the 24th, 11th, 1st, 7th, and 3rd Virginia) and Garnett's on the left (the 8th, 18th, 19th, 28th, and 56th Virginia). At an appropriate distance to their rear Armistead had ordered his supporting brigade, the 14th, 9th, 53rd, 57th, and 38th Virginia. In the center of each regiment the color bearers held aloft the regimental battle flags—the crimson fields bearing the starry blue "Southern Cross." Most regiments carried the regimentally marked flags issued to the division in June. Three, however— the 8th, 14th, and 38th Virginia—carried the older bunting battle flags that had replaced their silk battle flags and blue state flags in 1862.

Shortly after three o'clock, the division left their piles of blanket rolls and knapsacks and began the advance. For nearly 500 yards they marched straight forward toward the Emmitsburg Pike. Reaching that point, the regiments turned obliquely to the left, first for almost 300 yards and then, after realigning, for another 200 yards until they joined the advancing right flank of Pettigrew's leading regiments. All the while the Union artillery blasted them unmercifully. Once united with Pettigrew, the assault began. The stone wall still remained 400 yards from Pickett's command, and now canister and musketry combined to devastate the leading regiments. Stannard's Vermont brigade wheeled against Kemper's exposed flank, forcing his two right regiments to shift front to meet the threat while the others drifted left to avoid the murderous fire. Armistead had expected to fill the gap that should have widened when Kemper and Garnett took casualties and dressed center. Kemper's leftward drift, however, forced Armistead to deliver his attack through and somewhat to the left of Garnett's survivors. Hence, he now found himself intermixed with the remnants of Garnett's 56th Virginia and his own now-scattered brigade.

Leading a mixed throng of perhaps three hundred, including at least five battle flags from his and Garnett's brigades, Armistead surmounted the wall and surged forward at a run. Halfway to the crest, among the remaining guns and wreckage of Cushing's shattered battery, Armistead touched the muzzle of one of the abandoned cannons. At that moment, two bullets struck him, one in the arm and one behind his knee, and he staggered and collapsed. Without its leader, the dash was blunted, lacking both impetus and direction. Unable to break the line of the 72nd Pennsylvania at the crest, the remaining attackers drifted to the right, into the copse of trees that had been the focal point of Pickett's advance. Among the brambles, bloody melees ensued as the elements of Hall's and Harrow's Union brigades counterattacked to plug the gaps in Webb's brigade. But, when Armistead fell, the "high-water mark" of the Pickett-Pettigrew-Trimble Assault had been reached. Other individuals may have advanced closer to the Union lines, but for the Southern Confederacy the battle of Gettysburg was lost.

HOWARD M. MADAUS is the leading authority on Confederate flags of all types. He is the author of *The Battle Flags of the Confederate Army of Tennessee, Rebel Flags Afloat,* and *The Southern Cross.* He has written dozens of articles for various journals on flags and Civil War firearms and accoutrements. He is the curator of arms at the Milwaukee Public Museum.